The Ghost Detective series

Ghost Detective I: ISBN 978-0-9532563-3-4
Ghost Detective II: ISBN 978-0-9532563-4-1
Ghost Detective III: ISBN 978-0-9532563-5-8
Ghost Detective IV: ISBN 978-0-9532563-7-2

Acknowledgements

I would like to thank the following people and organisations for their input and assistance.

Dawn & Paul at the Moot Hall in Daventry.
www.pigeonholedaventry.co.uk

Members of Rushden Athletic Club and Institute.

Paul Beasley at the Royal Theatre in Northampton.
www.royalandderngate.co.uk

Margaret Holton, Greens Norton.

The Friends of Delapre Abbey (Front Cover) for their hospitality.
www.delapreabbey.org

1940's ghosts for the front cover were,
Martin & Lesley Littlejohn and Tracey Caney.
Members of the Northern Forties Group.
www.northernforties.org.uk

Book Cover
By
Maggie Needham
Brackley Photographic

Ghost Detective
V

Written
By

A H Perkins.

Paris & Wolf Publishing

May 2013

ISBN
978-0-9532563-8-9

Introduction

When you think how long people have been seeing ghosts and experiencing spirits you would think someone would have decided to find out how and why they occur. But it seems we are all still stuck in the dark ages allowing our superstitions to cloud our judgment. As for myself, I have formed my conclusions based on experience and my own interpretation of the events I have witnessed. The word, interpretation, has more meaning for the paranormal investigator than any other. When interviewing an eyewitness to a haunting, or indeed any strange event, it is their interpretation of what they have seen or felt that is the key to understanding the case. Their interpretation is formed from the individual's belief system. With so many different beliefs around the world no wonder it is so hard to form consistent conclusions. We know unexplained events happen to people on a regular basis, there is no disputing that, but to say they are largely ghost related is a step too far for me. I believe we have some abilities that we are just starting to understand, and others we have no knowledge of at all. In evolutionary terms we are just children playing with a toy we have little understanding of.

Do I believe in ghosts and spirits? Yes. But my interpretation of ghosts and spirits may not be the same as yours.

In each book I have written you can see how my experiences have changed my view on many subjects that are grouped under the paranormal banner. This is because I understand more than I did at the start. It's a bit like going to school, knowledge leads to understanding. Yet I still have unanswered questions about my experiences at Twinwood Farm in my second book. That experience is what drives me on and it will keep me investigating until I become part of what I seek.

Enjoy.

Ghosts of the Moot Hall

Set within the delightful Northamptonshire countryside is the bustling market town of Daventry. With many historic buildings and a diverse range of independent shops, I found the town a welcoming place in which to spend a few days. Some friends of mine, Dawn and Paul, had recently set up an antiques business in an empty building at the heart of the town. The building, known as the Moot Hall, is an impressive grade two-listed building dating back to 1769.

Dawn and Paul have had an interest in antiques for some time and moving into the Moot Hall was an inspired idea. The historic building in the heart of a town filled with antiques and collectables was just what the town needed. I popped in to see them as they were setting up the business and Paul invited me down to view the cellar, as you do. He knew I shared his love of history and this cellar did not disappoint. Five individual rooms of good proportion with arched pillars and flagstone and red brick floors, and two stone mullion windows below pavement level. We could have spent hours down there reading the structure of the place, but they had a business to set up and I also had an appointment to go to, but I would return.

I am always on the lookout for new places and new stories to investigate. So when I next visited the Moot Hall shortly before it opened to the public I was intrigued to hear that people had been seeing figures drifting along corridors and walking through doors.

Many of the reports were of a woman walking through the wall by the downstairs toilets, across the corridor, and into the toilet block. She had been seen on several occasions by three unrelated people. The reason for the ghosts route would become much clearer to me later.

On my next visit to the hall I could not resist going down into the cellar again; fortunately, I was with my good friend Lewis Dellar, my nickname for Lewis is Mole, for his love of subterranean caverns. I think Lewis loves cellars even more than I do so this visit would take a little longer to conclude.

On descending the stairway into the cellar there is a room immediately to the right at the bottom of the stairs, some fifteen feet in length, by about ten feet wide, and it has a red brick arched ceiling possibly eight feet high. Set into the back wall slightly to the right and about five feet above the floor is an opening to a chimney. The doorway into the room has large steel pin hinges heavily corroded over the years. The door to the room must have been of substantial weight and thickness to warrant such steel hinges. As we left the room and on examining the area just outside I distinctly saw a shadow moving within the room we had just left. Lewis tested whether it could have been our shadows reflecting into the room but we could not replicate what I had seen. We carried on investigating the other rooms without incident. We knew through the research our historian had carried out the Moot Hall was once a woman's prison. Maybe the fact that it was a prison holds the answer to why the cellar doors were so heavily built. One remaining door down in the cellar is of heavy steel construction, riveted all round and about one inch thick. This cellar is a puzzle and no mistake.

As word got out that we were investigating the Moot Hall another ghost story came to light from the building next door, the Plume of

Feathers public house. Nobody had told the people in the pub about the nature of the haunting in the Moot Hall, so when I went round to investigate their story imagine my surprise when the two stories matched up. Not only were the sightings similar, but when we were shown the point where the woman had been seen walking through the wall it was a perfect match to the corridor in the Moot where the woman is seen appearing. Now Lewis had an idea that the cellar in the Plume could have been linked at one point to the Moot, yes you've guessed it we were off down another cellar. As we searched the pubs cellar we came across two

First view of the heavy steel door in the cellar of the Moot Hall.

Photos above show the steel door in the cellar.

Below you can see the bricked up arches that matched the arches we had seen in cellar of the Moot. That was conformation right there, the two buildings did indeed once share cellars.

This is the cellar in the Moot Hall

You can see the two arches that once linked with the cellar in the pub. Behind the pipework in the centre of the picture is a bricked up fireplace.

I have a firm belief in ghosts being recordings of past events, and sightings in the Moot Hall are glimpses into past events, but we needed more information about the building to find out for sure. Our history researcher Tina was already on the case.

History of the Moot Hall by Tina Cockerill

Grade: II* Date Listed: 4 December 1953

12th c – The Priory of St Augustine established, originally at Preston Capes. Owned land around Daventry including the Manor.

1255 Daventry granted charter to become Market town.

1525 – Priory dissolved by order of Henry VIII and was given to Cardinal Wolsey who used its endowment to found Christ Church College, Cambridge. The land around the market, Abbey Street and the original Moot Hall had previously been owned by the priory.

Up until 1781 the estates were owned by the Finch family – Sir Heneage Finch Snr, recorder of London, and his son, also called Heneage, a lawyer during the time of the civil war, he became 1st Earl of Nottingham and was educated at Christ Church, Cambridge. The Land around Moot was split into small holdings now marked as Christ Church on the 1571 map and shows an orchard, yard and cottage. The orchard was mentioned in the 18c Tithing Report. The family also held the Manorial rights that included tolls of the markets & fairs, ownership of the Bake House and Malt house, and the old Moot Hall, which held the sessions room, gaol and butchers. Their 177 rents in 1669 gave an income of £564 11s 7d.

In the late 18c the Daventry estates were bought for £21,673 by a consortium consisting of John Plomer Clarke who later became High Sherriff, Charles Watkins (draper and banker) and three other prominent members of Daventry community. The properties were divided among them. Plomer Clarke also took the Manorial rights and consolidated his holdings in Welton Place Estate.

1752 Church of the Holy Cross built by David Hiorne of Warwick, both David and William worked for the Smiths in Warwick whose local projects included Lamport Hall, Kelmarsh

House and Cottesbrooke Hall. The Hiornes themselves built Arbury Hall, Guys Cliffe House and Meriden Hall.

1760 – First mention of Plume of Feathers – used by Millers of Daventry

1769 Moot Hall built as private house – possibly by Charles Watkins and designed by William Hiorne – although not officially attributed. It is possible that the front part of the cellars under the Moot and Plume were already in existence, maybe used as an undercover market. There are interconnecting arches in the front leading into the present Plume cellar, and in the Moot there are two large vaulted arches at the front below the present market, the ground level of the market may have been a lot lower. A house on the other side of the market square also has a cellar dating earlier than the building standing above it.

1771 – House occupied by James Riley a Draper, Banker and Insurance agent who in partnership with another had offices Shaw and Riley in the market square. It was not unusual for drapers to diversify their business, but in 1794 they were declared bankrupt.

The original layout of the Moot Hall as a house is unclear. Extensive alterations were carried out in around 1806.

A new body added to local Government sought that an Act of Parliament be passed. It gave them authority to clean up Daventry. It included what to do about the current dilapidated Moot Hall – The recently created Improvement Commission decided to pull down the existing Moot Hall and purchase another building. The new Moot Hall was perfect, not only was it right on the Market Square, it also belonged to Charles Watkins of consortium fame. Better paved streets which were drained, lit and clean, and a watchman or street keeper was employed to patrol the street removing beggars and keeping an eye on the public houses.

Markets & fairs were better regulated – meat could only be sold on the site of the old Moot Hall, and cheese from the market place at the new Moot Hall (possibly as previously described). Others were given specific areas to trade from. The trading times of the Market were also reduced from 11am till 1pm. The numbers of fairs was also reduced.

In 1806 the newly married John Plomer Clarke removed the staircase from the Moot Hall and installed it in the recently acquired Welton Manor. Not sure why this happened as the building was owned by Charles Watkins and not him!

The Cells were probably built during this time to provide a holding place to the Petty Sessions court and also as 'Lock-up'.

They were not used as prison cells as there was already cells in existence prior to the purchase and conversion of the old Abbey buildings, which in 1874 is described as 'good residence hall, 3 large cells and 2 constables'. It is probable that the back wall of the Moot Hall, now cottages, was a perimeter wall and that the cells were outside. During this time the Moot Hall had many uses. In addition to holding the Petty Sessions each Wednesday, during the nineteenth century the upper floors were offices for various businesses including the head office for a local smelting works!

1852 – Elizabeth Pinckard- was held after arrest of the murder of her mother in law. She was the last woman to be publically hung. After the trial her husband was left destitute and a subscription was set up, among the contributors was Mr Burton. It was also home to the Town Recorder, one family, the Burtons, provided three generations of town recorders. Edmonds Burton 1760-1820 was the first, followed by Edmond Singer Burton who incidentally married into the Watkins family, and Edmond Charles Burton who memorial stands on the site of the old Moot Hall.

The 20th century cottages were built to the rear of the Moot Hall in the late 19th or early 20th century when the area around it was called Corporation Yard. The first reference to the cottages was the 1901 Census when they were occupied, by William and Elizabeth Collins, and Henry and Martha Line. There was also a slaughterhouse in Corporation yard.

Now as you can see the Moot Hall has had a chequered past and it seems the cellar is much earlier than the structure above. The under croft theory is certainly one that would answer why there are substantial doors in the cellar. But what of the ghosts that have been seen. Is there an answer to why figures would be seen walking through the wall from the Plume of Feathers. It was Paul and Tina who worked out there was once a walkway along the back of the

Plume and the Moot, continuing through the wall and through what is now the toilet block. Both the Moot Hall and the Plume have been extended further back and now cover this walkway. The ghosts are recordings of people using the old walkway.

This investigation seemed to be answering some questions regarding the hauntings, but not all. Did the building hold spirits as well as ghosts? I intended to find out by an overnight investigation; this was agreed by Dawn and Paul and set up for the 24th of Sept 2011. Attending the investigation were Dawn, her friend Abby, Lewis, Judy, Tina, Mervyn, Michele, and myself. We have developed a new style of investigation, one where the medium goes in cold, no information whatsoever, no group following them around, and no contact with other members of the team, all they have with them is a Dictaphone with which to record their findings. Similarly, the historian holds all the history records on a location. Once the investigation is done all involved have a meeting to discuss their findings. We think by doing it this way both the credibility of the investigation, and those connected with it are maintained. However, on this particular investigation we could not use the new style as people already knew a little information and had previously discussed things. But never mind we were still going to give it a shot. Lewis and I had set up the cameras and we were ready to go. We started by having a general walk around, allowing people to relax and get a feel for the place. It is important to allow people to calm down. I still get a buzz on investigations after doing them for twenty years so it's important to be calm. After around half an hour people were starting to settle into the place and had started showing signs of awareness. By this I mean they were allowing their senses to do the work, listening, watching, and feeling for changes in the atmosphere around them. Lewis was the first to say what he was feeling. We had entered the first of two cells on the ground floor where prisoners were held on remand. The cells are a bit of a giveaway really due to the fact they still have the small barred windows by the doors. Lewis picked up on a man pacing up and down in the corridor immediately outside the two cells. He was holding a large key in what Lewis described as a piece of green velvet cloth. At the same time Lewis was describing this I saw a flash of light just outside the cell we were in, but nobody else seemed to see it. Lewis went on to describe the man as wearing black pointed ankle boots that flared at the top, his trousers were tucked into them. The man wore blue baggy trousers with a tunic to match, held together with gold shiny buttons. He wore nothing on his head and his hair was thin on top but was long at the sides. Lewis thinks the man had been in the clothes for some time from the state they were in. Judy asked Lewis if he thought the man worked at the Moot, a gaoler or something similar. Lewis explained he thought the man would not have held an important position and he was more likely to be a fetch and carry individual without responsibility. Judy then picked up on a large lady in a long skirt, pinafore, and shawl, a rather loud lady locked up for unruly behaviour in the street. Judy put the name of Mary to the woman she had picked up on. Lewis then had a name repeating in his head, Reginald Arthur, or Arthur Reginald. Michele, who was standing by Lewis at this time uttered words of surprise at this name. Michele is a carer for the elderly and one of her favourite clients was Reginald Arthur. He had died a few weeks earlier.

There is an interesting lesson to be learnt here. When investigating a property people assume that you will get ghosts related to it. Fair enough, if ghosts, as recordings, are seen then yes this is what you will get, but if you come across spirits within a property they can come from anywhere and be attached to someone in the investigating group. I believe this is the case here. Lewis thought he was putting the name to the man in uniform, when in fact he was experiencing two different elements at the same time, ghost and spirits, an extremely rare event through one person. It may have been Michele thinking of her old client which brought him forward as Lewis's thoughts were open to connect with him. This confusion was evident in Lewis's answer to a question Judy then asked him. Judy asked Lewis to ask the man what he wanted; Lewis answered unfinished business, adding the man did not look important enough to have any business. He was attributing the name to the man in uniform and not Michele's friend. At that point Judy pressed home her question, "What did the man want to say"? Lewis answered the man kept saying, "Shut up, shut up", Michele recognised these words as ones used by her old client. You see how this kept going back and forth? This contact seemed to disappear as quickly as it had arrived.

As different people described what they were picking up on, Tina thought it a good time to try to ascertain whether the two cells that were now in a corridor, were originally outside. The windows and original doors would point to this being the case but could someone sense, or see back in to the past. Several in the group thought this was correct and indeed the cells were at one point exposed to the elements.

It was now time to move to our next location in the Moot Hall, the cellar. On arriving down in the cellar members of the group each took a chair and formed a circle in the large room to the front. They did not intend to form a circle it just happened. When they had settled I switched off the lights and joined them. Again, it takes time to settle down and let your eyes become accustom to the light. I am a great believer in using your mind to see things. When you are in the dark why not close your eyes and allow your other senses to take over, even the ones you did not know you had.

Photo above shows the Moot Hall cellar looking back.
It extends under the building for some distance.

A general discussion started between members of the group regarding the age of the cellar. It is a way to divert your attention from the situation you find yourself in. This seems to work when you are seeking paranormal activity. Through experience, I have found if you wait for something paranormal to happen it won't, but if you go to a place where paranormal activity is said to occur and simply go about your business as normal, things start to happen in the background. What I am trying to say is don't try too hard. If it is there, you will see it or feel it, and you don't have to screw your face up in concentration to get results. The only time concentration is helpful is when you are seeking spirits, it is like an altered state of consciousness, or as a dear friend once said, a deep meditation. It takes practice and time, and I find solitude is the key for me. Anyway let's get back to the group.

On an earlier visit I glimpsed, in my mind's eye, an elderly gentleman lying dead at the bottom of the cellar stairs. The image was so strong I wanted to see if I could bring the image back and take a closer look. As the group chatted I closed my eyes and simply let my thoughts roam the building. It's a bit like walking about but you see with your mind and it gets easier the more you practice. As my thoughts came back to the cellar stairs the old gentleman came into view again. From his clothing I would date him to around the 1940's. He was lying on his side with his feet at the bottom of the stairs with his back to the outer wall as if he had just collapsed, not fallen, simply collapsed. He wore a white shirt with a slight off white striped pattern to it and the sleeves were rolled up. He was also wearing khaki trousers supported with braces, hobnail boots and a flat cap. Interestingly the cap was still on his head and had not fallen off as the old man had collapsed. I started telling the group what I was seeing and Judy asked if the man was inside or outside the building. Her theory is the cellar steps were once outside the building and that the cellar was an open under croft, a theory I support. But the man was inside the building at the time of his death. However, Judy's question sent my thoughts roaming the cellar, in particular the cellar steps and the wall to the right as you climbed them, or should I say the lack of a wall at the top right. My concentration broke as I tried to make sense of things. Lewis asked if I had a name but I had nothing like that, just the image. Then I realised Lewis was getting a name, he asked Tina if she had information regarding the pub next door. Tina has a list of the innkeepers going back to 1841, including their families. Lewis asked her to search for a Bethany Richards, possibly an innkeeper's wife. He associated her to the ghost of the woman seen in the Moot Hall.

A discussion then followed regarding the association between the pub building and the Moot Hall. Tina explained the footprint of the two buildings had changed substantially over the years and it is difficult to see today how the two buildings once looked. Time and alterations tend to mask the true nature of a building. At this point Judy was aware of someone standing behind her, slightly to her right. Michele asked me to ask out to see if we would get a response. I knew there was something with us but I did not know what it was. Even as I was asking for a response from whoever it was, a flash of light appeared to my left hand side. Instantly the group went into analysis mode and put it down to cars going by, but I think it was a bit too bright for that. Could Bethany Richards be listening to us? However, Judy thought the figure by her was that of a man. Lewis then saw a movement by Judy and asked her to move her left hand. She did so but he said the movement was not what he had just seen. The torso he had seen had light shading to it and a definite movement. The figure then appeared by Michele. It moved with such speed it would have been impossible for a living person to move so fast. Judy felt it was the spirit of a man who once worked at the pub who came back and forth through the arches that once linked the two cellars. Judy is convinced the cellar predates the Moot Hall, and I totally agree. Lewis and I then sensed and saw a shape bounding through a doorway away from the room we were in. It was a simultaneous sighting and one we both remarked upon.

Then it was Michele's turn to feel someone standing by her. She described a girl in shabby clothing, peasant like. While people were in such a state of awareness I asked them to visualise what they could see in the room with their minds. Lewis went first and said he saw a wide panoramic picture of a hunting scene, just the horses, riders, and dogs, no fox, and the picture was broken on the floor. Michele saw the floor of the cellar covered in straw with wooden benches dotted about and baskets of live chickens by the wall. I saw bright sunshine, as if someone was shining a torch at my eyes while they were shut, I could even feel the heat. Judy visualised a man in a white apron wearing a chef's hat. Everyone was getting something, apart from Mervyn and Tina.

This is not unusual in these circumstances. Let me explain why. Investigating ghosts and spirits is like any other subject you chose to learn about. Over time your knowledge grows with the experiences you have. It is easier to sense things when you have been doing it for a while, you get accustomed to situations others may find threatening. Tina and Mervyn had never been in a situation like this before and their reactions were normal. Tina then asked a very good question. We had all explored the Moot Hall room by room; Tina also knew its history. Her question was, "Where was the kitchen"? There wasn't one. Could the cellar have once been the kitchen? A discussion then began about what building was standing on the site of the Moot Hall before it had been built in 1769. Tina has maps showing the site was open land. A building did stand where the Plume of Feathers now stands but that was all. But the Moot Hall Cellar is older than the building above, that's the puzzle. We know a building across the market square has what we believe to be a cellar from a priory building and a stone circular staircase going nowhere. Could it be the Moot cellar dates back that far? The group were in real detective mode now so off we go to the next location in the Moot Hall.

The clock and attic rooms in the hall are a fair climb but one well worth undertaking. The clock, now converted to electricity, still has its original workings, for those interested in Horology it's a must see. The rooms opposite the clock room are connected one through another. They have been altered somewhat but I believe they were originally bedrooms, now used for storage. Slightly out of breath, all except Judy, we started exploring the rooms and discussing their functions. Judy was the first to explain what she was feeling. A claustrophobic sensation and one of being trapped was quite strong, possibly due to the low sloping ceiling. A discussion regarding servants quarters also came up and Tina was able to confirm the staircase was not as it would have been originally; the layout would have been much different. Two people picked up on children living up there and Judy thought they were trapped by a fire at some time in the past, probably 1843. The fire itself would have been localised, possibly in one room, and she thought possibly a nightgown caught fire by the fireside or even the child got too close to a candle. I asked if any names came into their thoughts, Tina would be able to verify names at the hall from particular times in history. Michele picked up an Isobel or Isabella but no surname. Judy got the name Daisy but again no surnames. Judy also got a date of 1714 but she acknowledged this did not fit with the history of the hall. Lewis then thought of a man standing with his back to the clock room with his arm raised holding what looked like a silver Colt pistol with a black handle. He put the timeline to modern day, as in the last 30 years.

After another look around upstairs we headed off for a break before our next location. We would be heading for the room on the second floor to the right of the stairs. During the break the group were trying to visualise the building as a home for a family rather than the business like structure you see today. Alterations made in 1806 have removed all clues to how the house once looked inside. Tina then noticed on the monitor a figure walk across the camera in the room we had just left, but all our people were accounted for. We knew from past experience it would be a fruitless journey to go back up to the room as there would be nobody there.

On entering our next location I wanted to see people's reaction to the room. Not because it was special, but I had told people we would be doing a circle there and their expectations would be heightened, it proved to be an interesting location. People started asking questions about the room and what it was used for and so on, I gave limited answers due to the experiment I wanted to do later. As the group settled down we were joined by one of the owners, Dawn, and her friend Amy. It was now evident people's expectations were indeed high; it's not a bad thing but I had to get them relaxed and ready to try an experiment. Turning off the lights the room took on a better atmosphere than previous locations that night. Now it was time to calm people down and get them into a relaxed and comfortable state of mind. You need to block out anything going on around you and focus on the room in which you are sitting. Close your eyes and with your mind visualise the room, empty, and then allow objects and people to enter the room. At first you are simply an observer seeing what develops. If you want to direct a question to a person you see come into your room then do it with your mind. Your observations at this time are crucial. I asked people to go deeper into their thoughts and walk about with the people they saw.

Before I tell you the results of the experiment I would like you to know my theory behind the test. Now remember at this point we are not trying to see ghosts we are trying to pick up on spirit. Not the mystical mumbo jumbo spirits people would have you believe in, but the natural spirit within us that continues after the body dies. Our conscious mind is bombarded with sensory overload during a normal working day. Sight, sound, smell, taste, and touch. As we relax at night our mind is as alert as it was during the day but we have less of a bombardment for our senses to deal with. We go to bed when our body needs to rest; we feel sleepy and need to recharge our batteries. As we drift off we are switching from one level of consciousness to another, eventually we drift into a dream state. Our mind is as active as ever but our senses are totally relaxed.

The experiment I use is trying to get to the point between being awake and being asleep. More seems to happen to people during this state of mind than at any other time. By replicating a state of mind we can observe people's reactions and experiences. So far people's experiences have been extremely encouraging and observations from people in this relaxed state have been proved to be correct and accurate. Now back to the experiment in hand.

After a decent time I asked people to start leaving the room their mind had created and to gently come back to the present day and be aware of the people around them. I went around the room asking for people's experiences and their reactions to what they had seen or thought. Judy went first and she had visualised the room we were in as a dining room with a large central table and dignitaries sat around it. There was a maid there who seemed to be of some significance and her name was Maria. There seemed to be a connection with one of the men around the room and Maria, possibly an affair or unwanted attention from Maria's point of view. Judy saw plates of food being brought into the room by servants and the word scullery was used, not kitchen. The scullery being a small room for washing and storing dishes and utensils and doing other kitchen chores. Could Maria have been a scullery maid? Later Judy wanted to do the experiment again for longer to see if she could locate the scullery. Lewis, although not being able to drift into an altered state of consciousness during the experiment did come up with the name Mary Butcher. The more you practice doing the experiment the better the results. Dawn saw a fireplace with the fire alight and an elderly lady sat by it with a small dog at her feet. Dawn is aware of the existence of a fireplace behind a wooden panel in the room. But as it was her first attempt she did well to get into the relaxed frame of mind allowing her to see the room in her mind's eye. Michele allowed her mind to wander the building, not concentrating on the room where we were, but she travelled back down to the cells and saw a large lady being thrown into a cell. Amy had trouble picturing the room without furniture; she could only see it as it is now. Tina felt the proportions of the room were wrong she could not shake the feeling that when the original staircase was removed the rooms in the house were fundamentally changed in size. I think she visualised larger rooms. Several people felt the rooms were too small. This sparked a discussion about how many changes have been made and how difficult it is now to read the building interior.

All in all it was an interesting night and enjoyed by everyone who took part. I did have questions that I still needed answers to and to be honest I needed more from the Moot Hall than I was getting, so I decided to do more. Lewis and I often do talks to groups, so we decided to give a talk at the Moot Hall about the work we do and what we had discovered in the hall. I also wanted to do some experiments with volunteers from the audience. As you may have gathered I am a great believer in the power of the mind and what we are capable of, now it was time to put it to the test. At 7-30 pm on the 29th of October 2011 we gave a talk in the Moot Hall. Such was the interest in Daventry about the talk that we were sold out two weeks before the talk date. On the day of the talk, cameras were set up to allow the audience to see live pictures from several locations within the building. The experiments I wanted to do would be in the following locations, the first cell, the cellar, the attic, and the room we had meditated in during the investigation. I had placed a pendulum in a side room in the attic. The pendulum was suspended in sand and I had set up a camera to do a close up. Nobody knew the location but the audience could see it on one of the monitors during the talk. Any movement from the pendulum would be seen and would leave a line in the sand.

The audience that night were extremely responsive and seemed keen to take part in whatever we had in mind. At the point in the evening when I asked for volunteers however, people were, shall we say, less keen? I then explained that there would be a minder with each individual at their location and I went on to explain what the experiments' aims were. In the cell we would test Expanded Memory Recall, similar to what we had done during the investigation where people are asked to visualise in their mind the room in which they are sitting, without any objects, just the room. Then they would be asked to allow their imagination to take over and see what entered the room. The cellar experiment would be the isolation experiment. Someone would sit in the dark trying to use their senses to contact spirits. The attic experiment would be the hardest test of all, the telekinesis test. You are asked to focus on three separate emotions, fear, anger, and joy. Each emotion would be given a good while to settle into, and a recovery time would be given between each one. The target for the emotions would be the pendulum people could see on the monitor. The aim would be to move the pendulum. A second telekinesis experiment would be done after the first had finished, and would be done in the meditation room I described earlier. Remember each experiment would be live on camera so the audience could see the results first hand.

So how did we get on? It seems women were less keen than the men on the first three experiments, all male. The cell experiment went slightly off course, but did prove interesting. The volunteer went further into an altered state of consciousness more than simple imagination could do. He was fearful of a spirit, so much so he recited the Lord's Prayer for protection. Now this was not the experiment that was called for and the minder was about to step in when things started to calm down and the person opened his eyes and regained his composure. Was the fact he was in what was visibly a prison cell a contributory factor to what had happened. Was his Christian faith his shield to whatever his mind was dealing with? Moreover, was the Lord's Prayer his solution to the problem? When he returned with his minder, I made sure he was ok before he returned to his seat. I also made a point of chatting to all the volunteers after the talk.

The cellar experiment went completely as I thought it would. The gentleman volunteer had no emotional hang-ups, was straight talking, and honest, perfect for the job. Take away mysticism and what you are left with is reality. He sat in the cellar and did his best to contact spirit through concentration. When he returned to the talk with his minder he said all he could feel was being isolated and cold. Interestingly. his wife is a medium. The attic experiment was the most difficult one to do. Luckily the volunteer was a young chap who wanted to give it his best shot. I had asked the minder to take particular care of the person during this experiment. The person being tested would signal when they had started each emotion, and when they stopped to relax. Now remember each experiment was on camera and was being observed by the entire audience. You could see the young man going through each emotion, but the pendulum did not move. I was not too surprised at the result as will become clearer later. When he returned with his minder the young chap was pleased that he had completed the experiment and done a good job, he got it right.

As I said before I was a little disappointed that all experiments were with men. I asked one more time for a volunteer, preferably a woman. The young man who had just returned was sitting in the front row with his mother and convinced her to put her hand up. Now this would be interesting. My belief is that women have retained more natural senses than men, no, let me rephrase that, women use their senses more than men, and men do not allow themselves to let go in the same way women do. When the hand went up Lewis looked at me and smiled. He knew, as I did, this was going to be good. Lewis led the woman to the meditation room and asked her to use her emotions to get some kind of response, allowing them to build and simply project them. While we continued the talk a pressure sensor in the meditation room went off. This is usually caused by someone opening or shutting a door in another part of the building, but we were all in the talk room and that door had never been closed, something was starting to happen. We could see the volunteer was allowing her emotions to build from the look of concentration on her face, and the fact she did not notice Lewis checking on her. Over the next few minutes the audience became distracted and pointed to the monitor, the pendulum was moving. This in itself was fantastic, but it was the way it was moving that caught my eye. It was drawing a square.

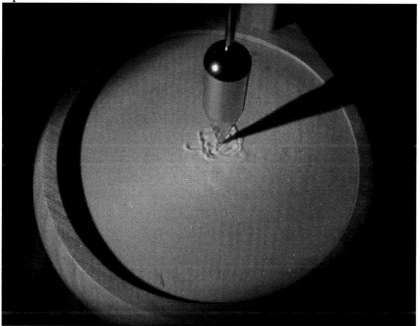

These types of pendulums are designed to draw intricate patterns in the sand, but not a square!

We decided to stop the experiment and bring the volunteer back. I chatted to her in a side room before she returned to the audience and she said she was not consciously trying to move the pendulum, she was simply trying to get something to happen, and she certainly succeeded in that.

My conclusions as to whether the Moot Hall is haunted or not? I would say it is haunted by ghosts rather than spirits. Don't just take my word for it, visit the place and see for yourselves.

My thanks once again to Dawn and Paul for their hospitality.

The Plume of Feathers

The Plume of Feathers is in the market town of Daventry, Northamptonshire. Sitting snugly between two larger buildings, the one to the left being Daventry's Moot Hall, and the one on the right being a modern build, the Plume is by far the oldest of the three. The first mention of the Plume of Feathers, used by Millers of Daventry, was in 1760. At the time of my visit the pub was being run by Chris and Dave. They had been running it for six and a half years so they knew every creak, knock, and bang the pub made. They had heard I was giving a talk in the Moot Hall and wanted to tell me about the ghost in their pub. Chris had actually seen a ghost in the toilets and another in the pool room, she also said the gas to the pumps kept being turned off, and when Chris sat on a particular stool behind the bar she often felt an arm put around her shoulder. Although Chris had seen a ghost standing by the pool table, Dave had seen it come in and go out through the wall that joins to the Moot Hall.

In his own words he said he was sat at the bar one night with a friend when he just happened to look up at the wall by the pool table and saw a ghostly figure walk through the wall into the pub. He doubted what he had just seen and wasn't going to say anything to his friend for fear of ridicule, but when he turned to look at his friend he realised his friend had just seen the same thing. Dave said to his friend, "You have just seen what I have seen haven't you". White faced his friend nodded and said, "Yes".

Chris said when she is a bit down and depressed, it's at that time she usually feels the arm around her shoulder, as in a comforting way. Over the years the ghost in the toilet has been seen by customers as well as staff. Ladies have been known to come running from the toilets swearing they had just seen a ghost. David said that glasses are taken off hooks over the bar and drop to the floor, some glasses shatter for no apparent reason.

I wanted to know more about the pub so I called on our historian, Tina, to try to find out who lived in the pub and when. Her results were outstanding.

The census records are from 1841 to 1938

1841
Samuel Peddlington b 1806 d 1871
Jane - wife b 1801 d 1854
Jane - daughter 1827
Joseph - son 1836
Eliza -daughter 1838

1851
Samuel
Jane
Jane
Joseph
Maria -daughter 1843

Maryanne - 1845
Sarah - sister in law
James Butler - servant 1826

Possible infant deaths, gaps between births.

1861
Samuel
Eliza
Maria
Maryanne
Sarah
William Ducket -servant

1871
William Barrett 1818
Abigail. - Wife 1818
Michael Downey - lodger 1850
Joseph Reddington - servant 1822
William went on to run the Swan pub on the other side of the Market
Place

1881
William Bezley 1840
Anne - wife 1839
Clarissa - daughter 1866
Albert - son 1867
Louisa - daughter 1869
Mary Anne -daughter 1870
Clary- daughter 1871
Daisy - daughter 1873
Ada - daughter 1877
Harry Hedges - son in law 1867 - makes him 14!!!!!

1891
Albert Collett 1843 d1911
Elizabeth - wife 1842
Edith - daughter 1871
Spencer - son 1873
Clara - daughter 1875
Edwin - 1877
Arthur - 1880
William - 1883

(Possible infant deaths, gaps between child dates of birth)

1901
Albert
Elizabeth
Clara
Arthur
William
Harry Sharpe -grandson 1896
Dorothy Sharpe - granddaughter 1897
Harry and Dorothy's mother is unknown. Harry was killed in action in 1917.

1911
William Biddell d1917
Clara Biddell formerly Collett d1935
Ida Collett Biddell 1908
Emily Mary 11 months
Edith Goode aged 20, servant

1938
Clara held the licence of the Plume.

Now for the observant among you some of the names may ring a bell. Some of the names were mentioned in the investigation in the Moot Hall. It was not uncommon for the children of families to be in service, and what better than to work next door. See how history can help identify people picked up on investigations.

I wanted to have a look down the cellar to see the arches that linked that cellar to the one in the Moot, Chris led the way. It was claustrophobic to say the least. Interestingly the ceiling was much lower in height than that of the cellar in the Moot. There were the arches, slightly hidden by clutter but undisturbed for many years. The only traffic through them now the occasional ghost retracing its steps. Chris felt uneasy being down there so we went back up into the bar. There is no doubt the pub is haunted, but by ghosts, not spirits.

Rushden Athletic Club & Institute

We travel now to the east of Northamptonshire and the town of Rushden. I had been told of strange happenings in a rather unique location.

Rushden Athletic Club and Institute is a fascinating building in itself and the people running it love the place. My first contact at the club was Lloyd, the current club secretary. We had had a conversation over the phone and he said come over and see what you can find out. So I went there the following Saturday to introduce myself and get to know people. Lloyd introduced me to Joanna, the vice president, who became my main point of contact for the club.

On my first proper visit in November 2011, I had arranged to do some interviews with past and present club officials and members of staff. I wanted to get a feel for the place, to get my head around why people felt so passionate about the club and its history. Their intimate knowledge of past events could shed light on some of the strange activity that had been reported. It's fair to say some people at the club viewed me with suspicion, wondering what I was up to, and I felt they were a little reluctant to give too much away. I understood this feeling and tried not to push the questions further than I thought the person wanted to go. Respect for the people you meet should always be given on any investigation. The structure of the interviews was as follows. I interviewed people about their knowledge of ghostly goings on. Tina interviewed people about the history. Tessie, our guest sensitive who you may recognise from previous investigations, tried to get a feel for the place by walking about and from what she was feeling. Lewis was watching people's reactions to questions and would pinpoint subjects that gave strong reactions. By structuring the visit in this way we covered a wide range of things in a short space of time.

My first interview regarding ghosts was with Stuart Brown, club steward up to March 2002. He knew the club extremely well and began by telling me about some strange events he had witnessed. He said he would often have a dog with him when shutting the place up at night and said when he went upstairs to switch off lights and make the building secure the dog would not go into the kitchen next to the stage, it would back away from the doorway. The same thing happened when taking the dog down towards the cellar; it would stop part way down the stairway and refuse to go any further. Also the lights in the ladies toilets upstairs would turn themselves on and off. Sometimes after work had finished Stuart sat having a drink with other members of staff and they would hear the sound of footsteps walking directly above them, interestingly that is the dance floor. Obviously they had to check it out even though they had just shut the place down. Each time they investigated the footsteps they found nobody there, but mysteriously the ladies toilet light would be on.

The stage and dance floor above the bar in the Club.

On other occasions the curtains across the stage would move as if somebody was walking by them. There is a small bar to the right as you enter the dance room and some years ago a barman serving drinks one Sunday dinnertime collapsed and died there.

View from the stage to the bar in the corner.

I asked Stuart whether he thought other members of staff were imagining things happening around them simply from the stories they had heard. Stuart said there must be something going on in the building because some people experiencing things knew nothing of the club history or past events. He also said these same events had been going on for years and people were so used to them that they were often taken as normal and not necessarily discussed.

I then asked Joanna about her experiences within the building. She had heard what she thought was a bouncing ball in the dance hall. She also experienced somebody rushing past her down in the cellar, but she said she could see nobody and the experience made her feel sick, so much so she had to sit down. She added that when she is standing on the stage in the dance hall she feels as though somebody is behind her waiting for the moment to push her off. I have to say when I stood on the stage I had a similar experience. Joanna had a very interesting photo to show me of a recent party held in the dance hall where the ghost of a child seemed to be joining in with the festivities.

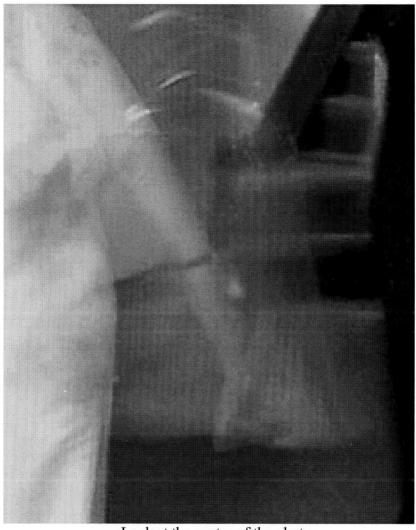
Look at the centre of the photo.

The woman in the foreground was having her photo taken, but there is a little girl standing in front of the stairs, sideways on. She is facing your left with her left arm holding a dress that seems much too big for her. Her left hand seems to be trying to gather the dress. She appears to be headless with a shaft of light coming from her shoulder. The steps behind her are the ones to the right of the stage.

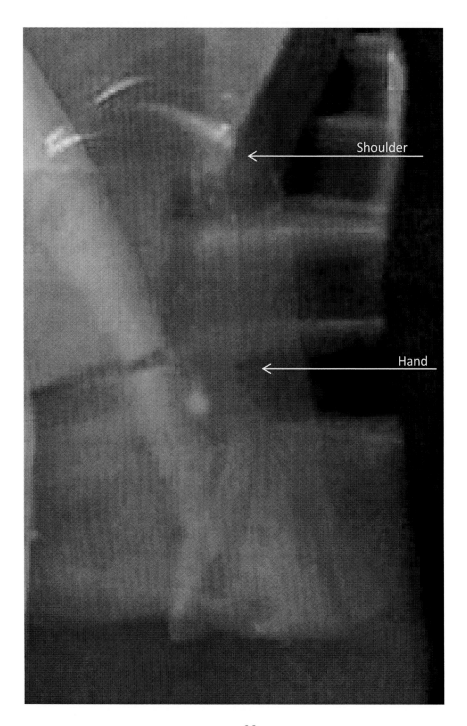

My next conversation was with Lloyd, and proved very interesting. His passion and pride for the club was very evident, and his knowledge of the club history was extremely good, but we will leave the history side of things for a little later in the story. Lloyd wanted to tell me what had happened while he was locking up the Saturday night I had first visited the club. He had locked the place up and checked to see that all was in order. His wife had walked to meet him and they were just closing the main door to leave when someone said, "Goodbye". Lloyd instinctively said goodbye in return and was about to close the door when his wife asked, "Who are you talking to"? Only then did Lloyd realise there was nobody in the club who could have spoken to him. He added he always feels uneasy and gets a cold feeling when down in the cellar.

My next chat was with Peggy. Peggy was a member of the yoga group, and part of a yoga class is learning meditation, and meditation can allow the mind to sense energy from ghosts and spirits. Other members of the group had already told me that they sense a female ghost in the dance hall. But Peggy had put a name to the ghost. She calls her Martha.

Many of the people I have chatted to in the club have been going there for over thirty years or more. Peggy has been going there for sixty years and remembers a time when she attended dance classes on a Wednesday evening and the social evening on a Saturday night. Saturday nights were extremely popular and Peggy said you needed to get there early in order to get your seat. The glitter ball that hangs from the ceiling in the dance hall is the original ball from the time Peggy remembers first coming to the club. She explained that on a Saturday night there was a cloakroom attendant called Martha who would look after people's coats and they would drop money in a bowl as payment. When Martha died anything that happened that was unusual was put down to Martha's ghost. Is it Martha that haunts the dance hall?

The dance hall had another surprise for us that evening. As I have already said Tessie was walking about the building trying to pick up on unusual energies from the past. While doing this she also took some photos of areas she thought curious. One particular photo taken in the dance hall was extremely interesting. The only other people in the dance hall at the time the photo was taken were two young children.

Photo above is Tessie's dance hall picture

It appears to show a shadow of someone looking through a window into the hall, possibly wearing a hat. But how can this be possible? The window in question is twenty feet up from the road. The next photo shows the location of the window in the dance hall.

The black arrow shows the window where the shadow was photographed.

There was enough activity in the club to warrant a full investigation with experiments and all the equipment we had access to. Tessie had walked around and identified areas where she thought cameras, pressure sensors, and audio recorders should be placed. We had enough equipment to go all out on this location so that's what we intended to do.

On the 3rd of December 2011 we set up our equipment around the club and had our control centre on the stage in the dance hall. The central people on the investigation were, Tessie, Lewis, Joanna, and myself. We wanted to keep a low profile during the investigation for two reasons; One, we did not want interruptions from the curious, and two we wanted people to go about their business as they would normally do. Things started really well and we decided to do some experiments to see if we could replicate some of the events we had been told about. Stuart had told us that a dog he had with him some years ago was reluctant to go into the kitchen by the stage, and refused to descend the stairs to the cellar. Melvyn Smith had agreed to bring his dog along for the investigation in order to see how it reacted to the two locations mentioned. Melvyn's dog was called Storm and was young, playful, and eager to search new places.

Here we see Storm having no trouble investigating the kitchen.

The kitchen upstairs by the stage proved to be no problem for Storm. There was only one moment when he stopped and stared toward the back of the room, but this was very brief and I think he heard something he was not sure of. Melvyn then led Storm down towards the cellar. Again the little dog had no problems.

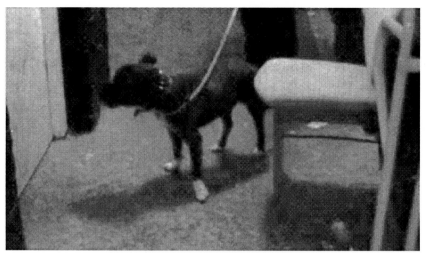
The cellar held no fear for the little dog.

I think there are possible reasons why Storm was seemingly unaffected by the location. Unlike the experience Stuart had with his dog, this dog was very young and very excited. He was also surrounded by new people he had never met before. I would imagine Stuart's dog would have been much older and used to the location. The place would have been quiet and deserted. We know dogs have much better senses than we do. It would be interesting to see Melvyn take Storm around the building in a couple of years from now after everyone had gone home. I have a feeling the result would be much different.

Now we move onto the human experiments. Mark is a regular at the Club and volunteered to do a Telekinesis experiment using emotion to move a pendulum that Lewis was monitoring on the computer screen. You may remember this experiment worked well on other investigations we had done. This experiment is extremely hard to do and requires serious concentration from the individual. Mark had his work cut out due to the noise from the club and from outside, but he was willing to give it a shot. I asked Mark to focus on three separate emotions, fear, anger, and joy. Each emotion would be given a good while to settle into, and a recovery time would be given between each one. The target for the emotions would be the pendulum Lewis could see on the monitor. Mark indicated he was ready and we started the experiment. Lewis would signal to me if movement was seen from the pendulum. I have to say I had serious doubts this would work due to the nature of the location. After some time I asked Mark to stop. It was clear we would not get a result from this particular experiment due to interruptions. Then something happened that was to throw all of us. All our video recording equipment went off, cameras, DVR's, everything. We checked the power and there was no reason for the machines to switch off and we could not get them back on. We were now down to one hand held video recorder and two audio recorders.

It was getting late now and people were leaving the club. Now the investigation could step up a gear and we decided to do a walk about to see if Tessie could pick up on anything. The cellar would be our first location. The cellar at the club has a full size rifle range in it and is in regular use by the club. Most of the time the doors to the range are locked but I did get a chance earlier before the club closed to go in with Joanna and she showed me around.

The rifle range in the cellar of the club.

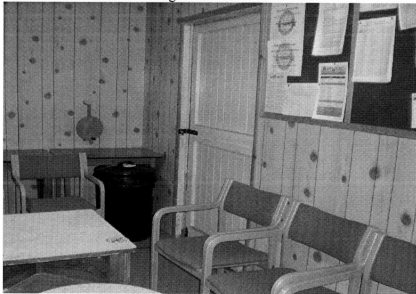

The door you see in the centre of the photo was the one Tessie was standing in front of when we investigated the cellar.

During our investigation, this room and the entire rifle range were locked and empty

From left to right Tessie, Joanna, and Lewis.

The extraordinary events about to happen by the rifle range in the cellar took us all by surprise. We could hear walking about upstairs so Joanna and Lewis went to investigate. Tessie asked if the spirit of Vincent was with us, Vincent was a local who had died, and on the audio recorder a female voice said no. We then heard thumping on the door behind Tessie, the door to the rifle range shown on the previous page. We both heard it and as Lewis and Joanna were returning it happened again. As soon as we tried to get another response it stopped altogether. We decided to split up. The girls would go up to the bar and see if they could get a response in there and I stayed down in the cellar with Lewis trying to get our spirit friend to make herself known again. All was quiet in the cellar for a while, and then suddenly a voice said, "Ade". Thinking it was Lewis I said what's up mate, but he had said nothing, and he never heard anything. We then heard walking upstairs so thinking it was the girls we made our way to them. But they were sitting quietly in a corner and had not moved. We swapped locations and the girls descended to the cellar. During their time down there they did not hear any voices but they did report hearing walking about upstairs. Lewis and I made a point of staying seated and did not walk about, so who, or what were we hearing? The cellar in this club is definitely haunted.

Later that evening the four of us decided to sit quietly in the dance hall to see what would happen.

Now we knew the building was secure and the only people in the building were Joanna, Tessie, Lewis and myself. What happened over the next five hours baffled all of us. We sat at a table to the side of the dance hall bar and allowed ourselves to become accustomed to the sounds and noises coming in from outside, cars going by, people walking home in high spirits, the creaking of the building as it cools down after an active night's festivity. All of these sounds must be eliminated from the investigation. I tested a theory that EVP's are best recorded when you are not expecting them, say during normal conversation. We just chatted between ourselves and we left our recorders on. During this time we recorded a woman humming, a man saying, "I give up", and a strange laugh. We also heard people talking and moving about down stairs, and the sound of someone walking on the concrete staircase that leads up to the dance hall from the car park. We saw nothing but heard countless other strange noises. Again, we decided to split up and see what would happen. The girls went down to the bar and we sat in the dance hall, again taking care not to walk about and the girls took the same care, so after a short time for them to settle down. Lewis and I were surprised to hear doors opening and closing, and it seemed to be coming from down stairs. In turn the girls were hearing what they took to be Lewis and me walking about above them. After half an hour or so we swapped places with the girls, and the same things were heard again. A distinct pattern was emerging and my conclusion is this. You hear a recording of what a person seated in a room would have heard. Say if you lived in a house and your neighbour played the trumpet loud enough for you to hear while you were in your living room. Years later if you and your neighbour had moved away and you had sold your house; the new occupiers of your house would occasionally hear a trumpet being played while they were in their living room. It seems the recording is only accessible to people listening in a place remote from where the sound was created and not in the exact place it happened.

Now for the history of the Athletic club. We know the land was bought in small strips over a period of time. As the club became more successful so they could afford to buy another strip of land to extend the building. Now don't think this was an easy task, it wasn't.

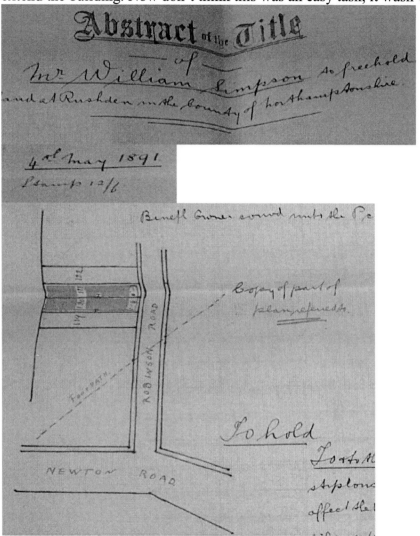

Strips of land acquired in 1891

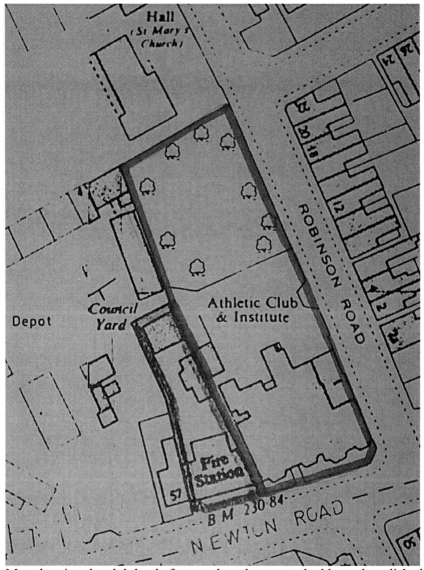

Map showing the club land after purchased property had been demolished.

The club once had a bowling green where the map shows a circle of trees.

We know that during the Second World War the club was used to billet English and American troops. As with all growing community buildings it has changed immensely over the years and people can trace generations of family who held office in the club. People often forget that without the enthusiasm from people like Joanna, Lloyd, and others, to do the day to day running of a club like this, with all its rich heritage, it would soon close, and that would be a big loss to the whole community. I found this investigation difficult to start with because people were a little reluctant to take part, but as time went on it turned out to be a real cracker. The club does have ghosts, but most are simply recordings of past events played back for those fortunate enough to hear or see them. There are two or three spirits from the past who enjoy a bit of mischief, but nothing sinister at all. Overall, it is a welcoming place and a great place to enjoy an evening's entertainment.

My thanks go to everyone at the club for making us feel welcome.

Eyewitnesses Stories

I am always on the lookout for new ghost stories from eyewitnesses. When the Hollowell Steam Rally was on in Northamptonshire I decided to attend for the two days and record peoples ghost stories. To say the weather was against us would have been an understatement, it was horrendous. Torrential rain and heavy vehicles turned the festival field into a sea of mud over a foot deep, but the atmosphere among those attending was superb. It brought the best out of people, each one helping the other to make the festival a success for all. The ghost stories came thick and fast, helped in no small part by the people on the public announcement system telling people I was at the festival with my old friend Lewis Dellar, to record their stories for book five.

So here we go with a rather chilling story that came from a young lady whose initials were P B, she was at the festival with her parents. While in bed one night, P had seen an image of her young aunt carrying a baby and smiling at her. She was not scared by what she saw as there was a great bond between the two of them. What she did not know at the time was her aunt had just been involved in a fatal car crash. At the hospital it was revealed the girls aunt was pregnant at the time of her death, but nobody had known, her fiancé said he believed even she had not known at the time. This information was told to no one. So how did the little girl see the mother and child? Was it a visitor from the afterlife?

Here are two stories from Janet Carter. When Janet was ten years old she was on holiday with her mum and dad in Caister, Great Yarmouth. They were staying in an old caravan, the type that had a dividing curtain. One evening after the curtain had been drawn Janet lay in bed and could hear her parents talking. Suddenly a lady appeared to walk through the curtain towards her. She was accompanied by two small children, one on either side, and all three wore white soft looking clothes. Janet noticed the woman had silver rings on each finger that were joined by a tiny chain. Janet sat up in bed and tried to scream but nothing would come out so she shut her eyes in total fear. Only seconds later she opened her eyes and the vision had gone. In the morning Janet was telling her father what she had seen and he said, "That's strange, look at my arm". He had been clawed from shoulder to elbow and as they were looking at it the caravan door flew open and the glass in it shattered. Interestingly there is a graveyard not far from the camp site. Was this a memory from the past? Now the rings are of interest, still sold today as a gothic fashion accessory. But they held meaning way back in history and signified slavery or bondage to someone or some group.

Jane lost her mum when she was twenty and this had upset her quite badly so she told her dad, whoever goes first come back to see the one left behind to let them know all is well. One night Jane lay in bed with her husband, who was snoring, when suddenly she saw her father standing at the bottom of her bed. He was dressed in his tweed jacket and trousers and had slippers on, he also appeared to be floating in mid-air and moving his foot from side to side. He spoke to Janet and said, "I have just come to tell you that your mum is alright and I am alright". Janet nudged her husband to wake him and said, "My dad is here" but when she looked back he had gone. Now Janet worked for a doctor and after she told him the story he said, it's all in your mind. Janet is totally convinced she saw her farther and it was a message they had agreed to give to each other after one or the other had died.

Here is Anna's story. Eighteen years ago her daughter was killed by a careless driver. Her daughters' cat always slept on her bed and from the day she was killed the cat would not go upstairs. Anna decided to take the cat upstairs to see what would happen. When she put the cat down it shot down the stairs as if frightened. The following Tuesday they had the funeral at the crematorium and two days after this the ashes were placed in the churchyard. Overall it had been about nine days from the crash to the ashes being placed in the churchyard. After the funeral Anna went home to get changed. When she went upstairs she walked passed her daughter's bedroom and there was the cat curled up on the bed fast asleep. Anna's mother saw her granddaughter in her hallway shortly after she was killed and described what she was wearing, right down to her boots. Now she couldn't possibly have known what the girl had been wearing on the fatal day but she was right.

Here is a story from Jackie White. Jackie once worked in a local nursing home in Northampton. One morning at about half six or seven o'clock she was wheeling a patient along a corridor in his wheelchair and she just happened to look into a room as she was passing that had its door open and she saw the wispy shape of a skirt gliding along the floor across the room. It made her stop and go back to have another look but it had gone. She told another member of staff that she had to go back into that room and she wasn't keen, the other member of staff said, it's early morning, and you probably imagined it. She knew she hadn't. But she went back upstairs to the room but before she entered she quickly put her hand around to the light switch. She carried on with her work and she never saw the skirt again. Around two years later she was on a nightshift with another girl she worked with occasionally and a bell rang upstairs. The girl looked nervous and asked Jackie if she would go up with her to see who was calling. Jackie asked why. The girl said, "You will only laugh at me if I tell you". Jackie promised not to laugh and the girl said, "One evening I went upstairs in the lift to answer a bell call, and when I got out of the lift I looked up to the banister above me and I saw, what I could only describe as a skirt drifting along the landing. It finally disappeared into the wall by the loft space". Now Jackie had never mentioned her sighting to the girl and a floating skirt is not your average haunting. On another occasion Jackie was attending to an elderly lady first thing in the morning and casually asked her if she had had a good night. The lady replied that it had been noisy with all those kids running in and out. Jackie said, "You have been dreaming, there are no children here". Jackie got the woman dressed and took her downstairs to breakfast and returned to attend to another lady in the next room. She again asked if she had had a good night and the lady replied, "No, bloody kids running in and out couldn't get a wink". Jackie started to wonder what was going on. She dressed the lady and took her to breakfast. The third lady Jackie went to attend was still asleep, but when she asked her if she had had a good night she replied, "Yes but who was the little girl who was kneeling in the doorway last night, has someone been bringing their kids in"? Jackie said, "No, there are no kids in here at night". The old lady looked puzzled and insisted the little girl was there. When Jackie looked into it further, where the lady's washbasin was there was an alcove, and years ago there was a door that led into a children's nursery.

Ghosts or spirit?

Here are two tales from Julie.

In Julie's first house which was built in Northampton in the 1950's they built an extension in the loft. One night at the time the work was being carried out Julie's husband was walking across the hall when he saw an elderly man walking down the stairs. They did a little investigating of their own and came to the conclusion it was the old gentleman who lived in the property before they had. They believe his ghost had been disturbed by the work being carried out in the loft. This seems to be a common factor in stories, when structural work is being carried out on a building it seems to release recordings from the past. We know recordings are sometimes trapped in structures. Many of these structures have been covered by modern plasterboard and brickwork. Is it the case that uncovering such structures can release the video of what once happened in the building long ago?

Julie's second story is about their second house. Their second house was built in 1902. A couple of months ago at about ten thirty in the morning Julie was stood in her bedroom. All the doors were locked and she was the only person in the house. Suddenly she heard heavy male footsteps walking along the upstairs landing, they paused for a second, and then she heard a door being opened and then closed. She tentatively opened the door and looked out, but there was no one there. Visitors to the house have also heard unexplained noises. They heard the sound of heavy boxes falling to the floor in bedrooms upstairs. When investigated no boxes, or indeed anything else had fallen over. Julie told her children there was nothing in the house that would hurt them. She is correct; it is again our old friend the recording. I hope you are beginning to understand just how common ghost recordings are.

Now here is a story from Jane.

When Jane was 14 years old her mother arranged a visit for them to go and stay in Jane's great aunt's house in Norfolk. Before they went Jane told her mother she would not go unless she could take her little bible. Even Jane admits for a fourteen years old girl to ask such a thing was strange. She remembers her mother saying, "Don't be so silly". But Jane said, "I mean it I am not going without it". So her mother gave in and she took the bible. Jane had never been to the house before so had no reason to fear it, or her great aunt, but the minute she stepped foot through the front door she knew she was being watched. Jane went up to arrange her things in her bedroom and felt so uneasy while she was in there. She kept a diary at the time and for some reason she put it between the pages of the bible. She said looking back she thinks she was trying to keep it safe. Jane shared a room with her sister and the family dog. When they went out to collect some fish and chips the dog was left alone in the house and went berserk, knocking things over and generally making a mess, very out of character. That night Jane woke for some reason and felt as though someone was leaning over her. She was lying face down with her head facing the wall and curiosity got the better of her so she stretched out her hand to see if anything was there. She was convinced someone stepped away from the bed, so with the confidence that she had forced them to step back she turned over to see who was there. She was confronted by a young man who stood about five foot two in height with short hair and he was wearing a light grey trench coat that was undone and black boots. He stared at her for a moment then turned and walked down the room heading for her parents room. She got up feeling unafraid and followed him. Once in her mum's room Jane thought about waking her to tell her about the man in the room, then thought better of it. Jane said because he was not solid, but then not really see-through, she somehow knew he was not a threat. After a few moments looking at her mother the man simply dissolved to nothing and Jane went back to bed. Interestingly her sister and the dog slept through the whole thing. Next day Jane told her mother that she knew the place was haunted for a fact, but again her mother repeatedly said, "No it's not". The next night Jane was awoken again but this time by strange laboured breathing. It wasn't her sister or the dog and her mother was too far away to hear her breathing. In the morning Jane said to her mum, I don't care what you say that house is haunted. Her mum said,

"Ok I give in, I did not want to tell you but yes it is haunted". She had seen a rag doll suspended in front of a window and heard an accordion being played upstairs. And she had seen the impression of, and felt, someone sit on her bed. When Jane told her about the man she had followed into her room her mother was, shall we say, less than pleased about it. Over the years Jane has had friends that have passed on and she has experienced things related to them so she has obviously a sensitive nature and picks up on activity quite easily. Thank you for your story Jane.

Here is a short story from Helen Philips.

Helen works in a private school just outside Buckingham. Many things have been seen and heard there over the years and Helen said one of the main rooms in the school that has activity is the dining room. People have reported feeling of being watched while they were setting up the tables, and on occasions the temperature seems to drop significantly. Helen saw a shape walk in front of her while she was in the serving area. This was not corner of the eye trickery, this was head on and close up. She thought it was her boss but on investigation she found she was completely alone. The lighting also has a mind of its own and comes on and goes off by itself. Children have also reported seeing a child sitting on a rocking horse in one of the upper bedrooms. Nobody seems to be able to identify the child and the sightings last for mere moments.

The Greens Norton Ghost

For our next story we pop over to the Northamptonshire village of Greens Norton. A small friendly place where people value the village way of life. Nestled down a side street stands an eighteenth century cottage. Once part of a row of workers cottages with gardens at the front, this cottage is a survivor from a different way of life many people crave for today. What you actually see when looking at the building is in fact two small one up one down cottages knocked into one. The owner, Mrs Margaret Holton, telephoned me one day and asked if I would be a speaker at the Greens Norton Wednesday club. While we were talking Margaret told me she had a ghost in her cottage and gave a brief account of the activity that she had experienced over the years. Intrigued by the tale I asked if I could arrange a meeting with her to discuss the story further. Margaret agreed and a few weeks later I was sat in her living room listening to a most interesting story. In fact the story was so unusual I asked for a further meeting in order to bring our historian Tina, and parapsychologist Lewis along. A little while before the second meeting was to be held I asked Tina to dig into the history of the location and see what she could find out. Lewis was invited due to the strange nature of the haunting; it was unlike anything I had come across before.

On the 23rd of August 2012 we all arrived at Mrs Holton's cottage and were warmly welcomed at the door. I had briefed Lewis and Tina on the story but asked Margaret to go over the details once more for their benefit.

Margaret had lived in the cottage for sixty years and had raised her family there. One day her young son Philip came down to breakfast and said he had seen a ghost sitting on his bed. Margaret told him not to be silly, but he was most insistent about what he had seen. He told Margaret he had seen a light float down from the ceiling and sit gently on the bed beside him. The light was as bright a day and instead of being scared of it he felt quite calm. He spoke to it and asked who it was, but received no response, and after a short while the light disappeared. A few weeks later he reported seeing the ghost again. This time it came from the ceiling and sat in the window, its brilliance was so great he could hardly see. It sat there for a while then got a little dimmer and shot off out through the window. Six months later Margaret's daughter and son-in-law stayed at the cottage. The first morning Margaret's daughter told her husband to relate the strange events that had happened during the night. Coming from London her husband did not believe, and had no interest in ghosts. He said if he had not witnessed what had happened that night he would not have believed it possible. He said that during the early hours he had been woken up by a bright light that filled the room. The source of the light came and stood by his bed and started hissing at him menacingly. He was petrified and shot under the bedclothes asking it to go away but it just kept on hissing. Eventually after what seemed like hours the hissing faded, and when he peered out from under the bedclothes the light had gone. He fumbled about in the dark searching for the light switch which he eventually found. It's strange how a light gives comfort to people when they feel scared. Margaret has a theory that her son Philip was friendly towards the ghost and in return it behaved in a friendly way. But her son-in-law, being a nonbeliever, and a little hostile toward the light, got a hostile reaction in return. Was it mimicking their behaviour? Or was it indeed giving its reaction to their feelings towards its appearance in the room.

The picture above shows the ceiling where the light came from.

Margaret has never seen the ghost but has heard what she believes to be a ghost, doors knocking and so on. A few days before this interview took place Margaret was going through her evening routine of making sure all windows and doors were secure. On entering the bedroom she saw the curtains had been drawn. Her first thoughts were someone had entered the house, but after a quick search she could find no one. Lewis asked Margaret if there was one location in the house that seemed to be more active than any other. Margaret said that the living room where we were sitting was the most active place in the house. Her little dog often followed an invisible presence around the room, jumping up in an attempt to play with whatever or whoever was there. Another curious thing that happened over some time was Margaret's previous little dog would go into the old bread oven and sit and lick the stone base. The dog licked the stone so much it actually wore the stone down.

The bread oven situated in the right of the inglenook fireplace.

Margaret's mother once lived next door and her mother's kitchen backed onto the bread oven and fireplace. Her mother always said that she believed there was something buried under there because when she cooked breakfast a man would walk out from the wall and walk past her. This happened so frequently she often said good morning to him, but she never got a response. Margaret's mother was interested in spirits and once at a meeting in Towcester her and some friends laid their hands on a table and asked the spirits to move it in answer to questions, the table floated and moved from one room to another. Margaret actually witnessed this happening. Today this is called table tipping and I have witnessed some interesting results at meetings but nothing on the scale that Margaret's mother had achieved. Margaret is not afraid of the ghost or spirit in her cottage. However, she is interested to find out why the spirit is getting so active lately.

Many years ago the house was altered inside and the staircase was moved and a bathroom added. One particular night Margaret was woken up by a loud crashing sound, as if the roof had caved in.

She immediately got up to investigate, quite expecting to find devastation everywhere. But to her amazement there was nothing out of place, all was normal. In the morning she asked her neighbours if they had heard anything during the night, but they had heard nothing. Margaret has a theory that the ghost always went about its business repeatedly going from room to room. When the staircase was moved she believed the ghost was unaware of the change and fell causing the noises. I believe something did happen at some time to cause the noise of crashing, but I think a spirit would have known about the alterations.

Now we get onto the history of the property and Tina had some interesting information and maps to share with Margaret.

In 1355 sir Thomas Green purchased Norton Davy for 20/-, dropping the Davy and adding the Green's.

Over the next centuries, the village was owned by Henry VIII (Katherine Parr was descended from the Greens) and stayed with the Grafton Estate until the mid-20th century when the Grafton family sold the village to help with death duties.

Our cottage was originally 2 separate, one up one down cottages, part of a row of cottages belonging to the Falcon estate. The date stone on the end gable of the terrace says 1671, and the original road lay out in front of the terrace was much different to how it is now. The road included another row of cottages to the south of Falcon Manor which had been demolished by the 1900's.

The cottages that belong to Falcon Manor (Falcon was added when Chessborough Falconer and John Macdonald, bought the Manor) and probably housed the families who served the Manor household and other tenants. 1911 census shows the servants as LAVELL, REED, GROVES, HARDING, BASHFORD, and MAY. The Manor was owned by several generations of the Pinckard family when in 1897, the last member of the family, Catherine, died. John Pinckard, husband of Elizabeth - last woman to be publicly hung in Northampton, ran the Red Lion pub in the village in about 1838.

The cottages were altered to make a larger family home and the road lay out was changed thanks to the Macdonalds in order to make access to the Manor by the household employees easier.

Margaret, the present owner, has had several strange things happen recently and she believes the activity is building and will come to a head shortly. She showed us up to the bedroom where the light had been seen. Curiously there is a large open cupboard to one side of the chimney breast in the bedroom that you can walk down into it. When inside the cupboard there also appears to be a banister of some kind on the wall to the right leading upward to the back wall of the property. In the same recess there appears to be a void to the back that has been blocked off, almost large enough to be a priest hole. But this was a workers cottage not a large manor house you would usually associate with priest holes. A puzzle indeed!

The investigation and activity in this cottage is on-going, as is the research into its past. For the history buffs among you here is a list of people associated with the manor.

My thanks to Tina.

Here is a list of servants that were associated with the Manor

1911 Manor Cottages

Henry Kirby, 1870 stud groom
Matilda 1871 wife
Philip son
Stephen son
Leonard son
Kathleen daughter

Williams Mansfield, gardener
Bertha wife
Harry
George
Mary
Arthur
Evelyn

The Manor
Chess Falconar Macdonald born Australia
Alice, wife
Claude, son
WT Falconar
Queenie
Margaret Guez, governess
Ross Smith, cook
Mary Chester, maid
Jessie Clapp, maid
Clara Phillips, maid
Genevieve Lagroupel, maid
None were born in Greens Norton, the family was from
Australia.

1901

No street name

Annie Taylor servant
Richards Bayliss, coachman

The manor
Chess Macdonald
Blanche
Queenie
Minnie Lovell, nurse
Annie Reed, cook
Emma Groves, maid
Edith Harding, maid
Ellen Bashford, maid
Kate May, maid, was the only one born in village

Towcester Road

Williams Mansfield, gardner
And family
Henry Kirby, coachman
Matilda, wife
Joseph
Philip
Winifred
Stephen
Leonard
James Haynes, gardener
Emma Haynes, wife

1891

Blakesley road

George Snelson, coachman and gardener
Elizabeth
Charlotte

Laundry Cottage
Anne Clarke, laundress

Manor house
Catherine Pinckard, own means
Maria Webb, companion
Sarah Bull, maid
Susannah Labrum, servant

1881

Blakesley Road

Spencer Longhand, fox keeper to Duke of Grafton
Mary
William
Frank
Alfred
Fanny

Park cottages
Jane French, servant
George Parker, groom

The Manor
Catherine
Louisa sister
Maria Webb, companion
Emma Charles, cook
Annie Sturridge, housemaid

4 Back Church Lane
George Snelson, coachman
Elizabeth

1871

Catherine
Louisa
John, brother
Letitia Franklin, niece
Elizabeth Snelson, cook
Charlotte Snelson
Ann Kirby, maid

Church Hill
35 Maria Thursby, laundress
36 George Snelson, servant, in 1861 was an agricultural labourer

1861
Manor
Annie Pinckard, head
Ellen Stanley, visitor
Charlotte Bowes, servant
Fanny Bowes, servant

Ann Davies, laundress
John Footer, groom

Further information discovered will be passed onto the local history group.

Helen of Soham

While collecting stories at the Hollowell festival I was invited, along with Lewis and Tina, to investigate a haunting in a house in Soham, Cambridgeshire. Chris and Wendy live in a delightful 17th century house on Hall Street. Wendy has lived in the house for about twenty years and Chris joined her some seventeen years ago. Before Wendy bought the house the previous owner had told her about the friendly ghost she had nicknamed Helen. Why Helen? Well, she had consulted a medium and the spirit had come through as Helen. Wendy was unfazed by this, in fact she was intrigued by the thought of having a ghost for company. The house was purchased and life was as normal as life ever gets. The odd bump and noise but nothing untoward. It was when Wendy's granddaughter Jamie came to stay that things became more interesting. Jamie was about four or five and regularly spent time at the cottage with Wendy. One day Wendy heard Jamie talking out loud, thinking she was talking to her dolls or an imaginary friend Wendy thought no more of it. Time went on and each time Jamie would visit Wendy could hear her talking away to her friend. One evening Wendy went up while Jamie was talking and she looked into the room, the little girl was not talking to her dolls, or indeed anything she was actually playing with, she seemed to be talking to someone without actually looking at them. Wendy asked her if she was alright Jamie replied, "Yes, my friend Helen is cold so I am going to let her wear my sweater because she needs one". Wendy thought Jamie was talking about someone at school and said alright my dear. It was only later she realised she must have been talking about the ghost Helen. Chris put Jamie to bed one night and was about to lay her teddies next to her when she said," No don't put them there, Helen my friend is laying there". Chris said," Alright I will put them in the corner", not wishing to make an issue of it. Jamie would let Chris lie on the bed to read her a bedtime story or just to give her a cuddle, but after Chris got up that was it, it was Helen's place to lay down. This carried on for five years or so, and then there was a break for about four years and in that time Jamie did not stay with them.

When Jamie returned she would not go into the bedroom. She loves staying at the cottage but refuses to go into her old bedroom. Wendy asked her why she would not sleep in her old room, and Jamie said, "It was the dolls". Wendy said she would remove the dolls but Jamie still refused to stay in there. Strangely one day Jamie brought a friend home to play and they went up and played in her old room. Wendy thought this was most odd, knowing how much fuss she had made about not staying in there. So when her friend had gone Wendy asked Jamie what was different about playing in the room today and not wanting to be in the room on other days. She simply said," I wasn't alone today; I don't want to be alone in there". Now while I was listening to Chris and Wendy telling me this story Lewis and Tina were also in the room listening and taking notes. Lewis made an important observation about the behaviour of the ghost, and of Jamie. It is easy to think of the ghost as a woman. But when you look at the evidence it seems there is no motherly type of behaviour coming from the ghost, just childlike friendship, playing with toys, chatting and lying next to one another. After the break of visits, on her return Jamie is that much older and her ghost friend has stayed as she was. You can understand Jamie's fear. Wendy said Jamie will only sleep in their room in a sleeping bag at the bottom of the bed. But there are more than two bedrooms in the house. Lewis thinks the fact that Jamie will now only sleep in a sleeping bag in the same room as Chris and Wendy it obviously means Helen's ghost is not confined to one room. This fact was now to become clearer as the conversation continued. Wendy and Chris are thinking of moving house. It is much too large a property for the two of them on their own and the house takes a great deal of maintenance. After they had made this decision Helen the ghost seemed to become more active. Not in a malicious way, but more in a mischievous one. This cements our theory that we are dealing with the spirit of a child here. The escalation of activity was noticed when things began to go missing, then would suddenly reappear as if by magic. Chris could not find his glasses one day and was forced to drive to Bedford in prescription sunglasses. Now this in itself you would think was not too bad, but the glasses went missing the day Wendy and Chris had to drive to Bedford Steam Rally, at four o'clock in the morning and they would be there for two days. When they returned the glasses were where Chris always put them. Chris once had a window cleaning business and had a big brass wiper with a rubber blade to run over the glass while he was cleaning the windows. He always put it in the same place when he got home along with the other equipment. One morning as he was about to go off to work he went to the cupboard but the wiper was nowhere to be seen. It was several days later when Chris went to the cupboard to get his equipment, and the replacement wiper, there on the shelf lay the old wiper as if it had never left. Wendy also had a pair of slippers go missing and to this day they have never reappeared. She has two cats that on more than one occasion seem to sit and follow an unseen presence around the room.

We had arranged with Wendy and Chris to spend the night with them and to monitor any activity that happened throughout the house. After listening to the story Tina would spend the night in Jamie's old room while Lewis and I took another room to use as a monitor base for the many recording pieces of equipment we had brought with us. I had four trigger objects with me. These objects were placed around the house in order to tempt our collecting ghost. We had a man's watch, a woman's brooch, a toy plane for a young boy, and a pink sparkly bangle for a young girl. This we hoped would cover all eventualities regarding age and gender. We also had CCTV cameras in position to monitor these objects. A voice activated tape recorder, a night vision hand held video camera, and pressure sensors completed the setup. The pressure sensors were there to monitor pressure build up in rooms where doors were reported to open by themselves. All was set and we settled down for the night. It started of quietly, as we thought it might. Lewis and I heard two loud thuds from directly below our bedroom, and forceful enough to cause vibration through the bedroom floor, but the monitors reported nothing. Later I went out on the landing after hearing the floorboards creaking on the stairs and noticed Tina had put her light on and had the bedroom door open. Not wanting to wake her, I decided to back into the monitoring room.

Apart from some power fluctuations, there was nothing to be seen on the cameras. After a while I dozed off into a sound sleep. Suddenly I felt a cold hand wipe across my forehead from left to right. It startled me so much I let out a cry that made Lewis jump and grab his camcorder. "What the hell" he shouted. I shot up so quickly I nearly fell off the bed. I was frantically trying to see what it was in the room that had touched me. Lewis was about six feet away from me in a sleeping bag trying to film and asking me what had just happened. The hand that had stroked my forehead had been quite forceful and extremely cold. I could not tell if it were male, female, or child, but it certainly took me by surprise. Lewis said we should check on Tina so I went out along the landing toward her room. The door was still open and the light was on. Tina was lying in bed inside her sleeping bag with the hood up reading a book. I asked if she was alright and she said, "Sort of". She seemed a little scared so I invited her to join Lewis and me in the monitor room. Once there Tina explained she felt as if the dolls were looking at her. She actually went over to the dolls and turned them all around so they were not looking at her. She could not sleep with the light on or off so had decided to read. She had heard something moments before I had gone to see her but could not tell what it was. Lewis told her what had just happened and I don't think that made her feel any better. We decided to stay in one room and settled down to sleep, all but me, I had decided that I would stay awake the whole night, whatever it was it wasn't catching me off guard again. I watched the monitors for the rest of the evening and watched both of my companions have a restless night's sleep. As the morning came and light grew in intensity, our room seemed very normal and the events during the night seemed a distant memory and quite trivial. We heard Chris get up and decided to start packing away the equipment. At breakfast we told Wendy and Chris what had happened and neither of them had experienced anything like that in the house. I felt the house still had secrets to be uncovered so with permission from Wendy and Chris we would look into the history of the property. Maybe we can find answers to who the little girl is and why she haunts the house. Wendy and Chris told us that they sat and told Helen the ghost that they wanted her to join them in their new home when they moved. Since that time Helen has been quiet. Tina could find no information about the property apart from the possibility it may have been a public house at one time. What you do not see from the photo of the house is the way it is constructed. Imagine an old plaster and black beam house like the ones you see in Stratford-Upon- Avon. Well that's what this house once looked like under all the modern render. My thanks to Wendy and Chris for their hospitality and I would love to go back one day.

The Royal & Derngate Theatre

Paul Beasley is head of workshops at the Royal and Derngate theatre in Northampton. He had invited me to the theatre to show me around and tell me about the strange activity that happens from time to time. This is his story. One of the walls in the main workshop once backed onto the old bus station, another is called the garden wall, and one was the back of the old paint shop. This area is the oldest part of the theatre and the eeriest. One night Paul was in the workshops at the back of the theatre. This particular night they were working on a pantomime and were really behind so had to work all night in an attempt to catch up. At around two in the morning Paul decided to go and have a cup of tea. Now to get to the tearoom from the workshop you needed to go down some steps, one of them being an old gravestone. On returning to the workshop after a break he saw the bench, some ten feet long by eight feet wide and solidly built, lifted off the floor, shook violently and crashed back to the floor creating a cloud of sawdust.

Above is a photo of the carpentry workshop bench.
The photo hangs in the workshop and has suffered from a little paint splashed.

On seeing this Paul decided to go back and have another cup of tea while he tried to make sense of what he had just witnessed. He added that there had been a period of intense activity some time ago now when the accident rate went through the roof, actors falling off the stage, people being injured in the workshop and so on. Rumours started circulating about ghosts and spirits not being happy with the alterations and recent refurbishment that had been done; so much so a medium was allowed to roam the place so see if she could sense a presence. The medium picked up on several energies, one being the heavy presence of a young girl called Louise at a particular point on the stage. Interestingly Paul had a cousin who died at the age of thirteen shortly after he had shown her around the theatre, and her name was Louise. Another strong presence was that of a man below the stage by the trap door. Actors have often reported seeing ghosts in the box to stage left. Paul added that this was the most frequently reported sighting from the stage. When rehearsing the actors would see figures watching them from the box.

The photo above shows the haunted box.

Photo above is a view from the stage. The ghost of a lady has been seen in the circle on more than one occasion.

The old master carpenter, Brian, sadly no longer with us, worked his way up and eventually became the front of house manager. In the early eighties while he was walking through what is known as the circle, clearing the house at the end of the night, he saw a lady standing there. He explained what he was doing and politely asked her to leave and to his astonishment the woman simply turned, walked to the end of the row of seats, up a step, walked straight through the wall and disappeared. To say he was stunned would be an understatement.

Paul Beazley standing close to the spot where the grey lady has been seen on more than one occasion.

I am no longer a believer in orbs but the orb in the photo above is at the position where the woman was seen, coincidence? To the left of the pillar behind Paul is where the lady walked through the wall. Paul also explained that during a recent refurbishment to the theatre a body had been dug up from the foundations, this was also at the time of the heightened activity I spoke of earlier. Paul then took me below the stage and showed me the entrance to the orchestra pit where the medium picked up on the energy of a male spirit, I found it very claustrophobic.

Paul then showed me this painting by Tom Osborne Robinson.

He had been a designer at the theatre and a well-known artist. The story goes that while the theatre was closed down for refurbishments they hung curtains over the painting. The medium identified the painter as one of the troubled spirits. After refurbishments had been done the curtains were taken off and things calmed down. It is said if the painting is ever covered over again bad things would befall the theatre once more.

To get a feel for how things worked off stage during performances Paul took me up into the gantry above the stage.

Photo above shows the view down from the top Gantry.

I asked Paul if accidents were common while people worked above the stage in the rigging. He explained that people who worked up there were so safety conscious there were surprisingly few accidents there. While I was up there it was almost like being aboard a tall mast sailing ship with all the rigging and rope work. Paul explained the Royal was among the few theatres that still worked with the rope system. In the next picture you will see what I mean.

You need to know what you are doing up there and that's a fact.

Descending back down to the stage Paul explained that the theatre is a place that people love. Whether working there or watching shows over a period of years people fall in love with the place. Theatres are also places of superstition and traditions that go back centuries. As a believer in ghosts and spirits I find the possibility that after death people elect to visit the place where they have loved working and visiting quite normal.

The Royal is a place that Northampton should be immensely proud of. If it ever closed Northampton would lose more than just a theatre, it would lose a big chunk of its heritage.

Thank you for showing me around Paul.

Ghosts of the White Hart

On the 20th of August 2012, I met my good friend Judy at the White Hart pub in the village of Flore, Northamptonshire. The village lies about three miles west of junction sixteen of the M1. Tales of hauntings had been reported for years, but were they true? Judy and I were about to do a preliminary search of the location to see if it deserved a full investigation or not. At the time of our visit the pub was undergoing renovations and had a caretaker manager, Tom, behind the bar. Now Tom was a great believer in ghosts so he was keen to show us around the property. But before he did I wanted to hear what had been happening in the pub.

Tom began his story by explaining that he thought the spirit in the pub was playful rather than evil and he did not mind the games the spirit got up to. At one particular point on the bar there are four bar taps called a 'T' bar. On the front of the taps there are plastic advertising badges held there with double sided tape. If the beer brand changes you simply remove the old badge and replace it with the new brand. Tom would be working in the bar and would hear a snapping sound. On investigation he would find the plastic badge to one of the taps lying on the bar. He would click it back in place and just to be sure it was firmly positioned he would hit the bar or the pump to see if it would fall out. On walking away he would hear a snap again and turning round he would find the badge lying back on the bar. One day while the pub was closed Tom entered the pub by the back door and while walking through the bar he said "Come on then let's see how good you are, throw that badge over to me". With a loud crack the badge came hurtling toward him and fell to the floor by his feet. He said "Well done, I am impressed", he picked up the badge and stuck it back on the tap and carried on with his work without further incident.

Tom was speaking to the girls who serve in the pub and told them he believed the pub to be haunted. As he did this there was a snapping sound and Tom told the girls the ghost had just put a badge from the beer tap on the bar. The girls looked and sure enough the badge was where Tom said it would be. They accused him of doing it and Tom said, "Ok believe what you want" and stuck the badge back in. During that evening the girls had to stick that badge back in on several occasions. Curiously after closing hours the badge stayed put. Eventually the tap was thrown out and ever since then there has been an uneasy feeling behind the bar in that particular place and many people have remarked upon it.

During the pub renovations Tom had lost tools never to see them again. Other tools were moved to a different room to the one he had been working in. Tom would often ask the spirits to bring his tools back, and within minutes he would stumble upon them in a completely different part of the building.

Led by Tom we decided to have a good look around the pub. I wanted to explore two things, firstly I wanted to gauge people's reaction to different parts of the building, and secondly were there alternative answers to some of the phenomena reported over the years. Judy knew the building well but had not been in the pub since the alterations, this would prove useful. Tom led us to a large open area to the back of the pub. Judy identified this as the north facing yard, toilets to the back and a staircase to the right leading up to the function room. The yard had been covered over by a roof and was used as a seating or games area. We were led across the yard to the entrance to the cellar. Steep steps led down to a damp vaulted room with another large room leading off to one side. Tom explained that the cellar had not been used for many years due to flooding. He went on to explain that a good cellar pump would bring the cellar back into a serviceable part of the pub once more. Because the cellar was dark and damp stories of it being haunted had spread, and people were dared to go and spend some time down there. The slightest sound would send them running and screaming out and the ghost story would be strengthened, many stories begin in this way. Interestingly reports of strange sounds being heard while people were sitting by the large open fireplace of the pub had been reported for many years and the cellar is directly below the fireplace. Another reason why the cellar is disused is the brewery can't deliver beer to it. The cellar head where the barrels would be dropped down would normally be outside the pub. But over the years the pub has been extended and the cellar head is now covered over and is inside the pub.

Tom then led us up to the function room, sadly no longer used. Judy remembers this as one large room with parties and wedding receptions. The large room has been split into two smaller rooms and is now used for storage. A strange smell I recognised from my days in secondary school filled the air. It was the smell of waxed wooden floors you used to get in large assembly halls. Maybe the floor in this old function room was once polished and waxed and it was this memory I could sense. While I was recording the conversations between people up in the function room, the microphone had recorded the sound of someone stroking it as if it were a pet dog or cat, it was quite distinctive and very strange, I was holding the microphone and I could feel and see nothing. An access way has been built that allows access back to the pub from the function rooms and leads directly to the pub's living quarters, bathroom, kitchen, bedrooms, and living room. Tom has never experienced any paranormal activity in these rooms, and said he has never stayed overnight in the pub and has no wish to.

Back downstairs we went outside to explore the outbuildings, they seemed to be old stable blocks that have been converted to a pub cellar. Tom renovates pub properties for a living and in haunted pubs he often does séances before he leaves to find out who the ghosts are.

We decided an investigation would be a good idea and one was set up for the following week. People attending the investigation were, Judy, Lorna Judy's sister, Tina, Viv, Lewis, Tom, and myself. Tom gave a short description of activity he has experienced for those who were not on the first visit. The pub felt different somehow, I couldn't put my finger on what it was but the atmosphere was different. Judy and her sister knew things about the pub that nobody else knew that night, and it would be a good test to see if anyone could pick up on information that they could verify, names, events, and so on. Tina, who is our historian, had maps of the village and of the pub from 1825 and 1885, showing its layout. The main structure is much as it was but the houses that are now attached to the pub were detached. The pub has grown with time and the internal layout bears no resemblance to the original. Tom began his tour of the pub for the people who could not attend the first meeting. I wanted to see people's reaction to the different parts of the building. Up in the function room I began to feel a severe headache starting. Judy wanted to sit in the room quietly for a while without disturbance and I asked people to stand quietly and relax. After a while I asked them to do the Expanded Memory Recall experiment. It's an experiment I came up with that seems to work. You memorise the room in which you are standing, just the room not the furniture or fitments, just the structure of the room. You then allow your imagination to fill the room with whatever comes into your thoughts, and allow the thoughts to develop. The experiment is to see if people can tune into events from the past. I have had great success with it in the past and from people who do not believe in ghosts or spirits. People's imagination is so complex we are just starting to discover its true potential, and sometimes what you think you imagine is actually fact. Lewis was the first to see images in his mind, but they were outside in the car park not in the room we were in. He could see people sat at a long table set out for a party and the place was covered with union jacks. Judy was seeing a baby in a cot. Lewis distinctly heard a moan sound and asked us if we had heard the same thing but nobody else heard anything. Interestingly it was picked up on the recorder and continued for about fifteen seconds while we were talking about it. The EMF meter suddenly sprang into action and with a spike reading seven and then disappearing just as suddenly. Judy then came up with the name William Ayres. Lewis then said he had in his mind the picture of a small boy on a peddle tricycle in what is now the pool room. The boy was wearing a flat cap and was very well dressed, (Sunday best). That part of the pub is an extension and would have been an open yard years ago. Strangely during the recording of the investigation my voice became distinctly lower in tone, I did not recognise my own voice on the recording at one point. In a distant room I heard the sound of a girl giggling; this was confirmed by Lorna and Tom who also heard the voice. There have been tales of ghostly children playing within the pub, but not upstairs. I was getting voices on the recorder that seemed to be having a conversation of their own and the people around me could not hear them. I know Judy was trying to tune into the spirit of a female and she believed the spirit was interested in what we were doing. Was it the same spirit on the recording? We had recorded this kind of phenomena before and it seems to come through when recording white noise. White noise is the background hiss you get on most recorders.

We all moved to a small room, possibly a bedroom, and Judy picked up on a baby boy in a cot and thought the female spirit was looking for the boy. I then recorded a knocking sound in the room but to my surprise nobody else heard it, and as I asked people to stand still a girl's voice said, "Why". Then three of us heard knocking from way down the corridor. Lewis went to investigate to see if there was someone else in the building. He returned and said he could find no reason for the noise, as he was talking the sound of glasses knocking together came from somewhere behind him and was instantly heard by four people in the group. This night was gearing up to be something a little special. What happened next definitely took me by surprise. Lewis saw someone's head on the staircase go from left to right as if rounding the corner to come up the staircase. He described it as a dark shape but distinctly being a human head. We moved further along the corridor to another small room. I hung back slightly with Tina and was explaining about how buildings create their own sounds when

Tom said, "That's just Adrian coughing in the next room". Lewis told Tom I was back along the corridor with Tina. Tom thought I had gone into the next room and it was me coughing, again several people heard the sound. Tom actually looked into the room to ask if I was alright, that's how convinced he had been.

Things began to quieten down over the next half an hour and it gave us time to explain to people within the group how electrical impulses from mobile phones and the electromagnetic fields from electrical goods can affect people's senses. It seemed a good idea while things were quiet. Later we went downstairs, and down to explore the cellar. While we were all down there Tom explained that years ago some young children were playing there and when called for their dinner by their mother they took a long time to arrive. She asked what had taken them so long and their answer was they had been talking to an old man who was in the cellar. Worried by this the mother went down the cellar, thinking a tramp or someone was down there and had been there with her children. But when she looked there was nobody to be found. Lewis remarked on the state of my voice when I asked out for a reply from the spirits. On the recording you can hear it had gone far below the depth of voice I could normally reach, very strange. We could sense nothing in the cellar and went back upstairs to regroup in the bar and to sit in circle, our final push to contact the spirits of the White Hart.

We had not planned to do a meditation circle but owing to the nature of the investigation, and the difficulty some were having experiencing the activity that had happened I thought it would be helpful. Judy led the proceedings and explained what we would be trying to achieve. By helping people relax and reach a state of calm within, it gives an individual a chance to experience an altered state of consciousness; in this state it is sometimes possible to receive guidance through the energy of spirit. Some call it self-awareness; others say we drift close to the spirit realm. Whatever your belief, it often delivers results. For myself I find it difficult to relax and feel a reluctance to let go and drift into that final state. Experience has taught me not to explore to deeply into the abyss unless you have a safety line attached to get you out, but that's just me. Judy asked those who had never tried this deep meditation before if they were comfortable with it, all were in agreement. The lights went out and we were ready to begin. Judy asked us to sit quietly and still and allow ourselves to slowly relax and concentrate on our breathing. Shut everything else out and just concentrate on yourself and how you feel within. After some time Judy asked us to let our muscles start to relax, starting with the face, down through the neck, arms, and chest, like a warm glow drifting down through the body to the feet. She then asked us to imagine a beautiful place, a sunny beach, a shady spot by a slow moving river, any place where we felt happy and peaceful. Somewhere within this beautiful place you see a bench or seat. As you wait you see someone, or several people approaching, and they sit on the seat. Talk to the people and see what you can find out about them, or what they have to say to you. Before Judy stopped talking she said she would leave us for a while to get to know the person we had met and to hear what they had to say to us. At that point one of the group felt sick and had to go out for some air. After some time Judy slowly brought us back to being aware of our surroundings and we began to discuss our findings.

Tom saw his parents in the place he went to and said he told them all the things he had wanted to say to them while they were alive but didn't, and they said they already knew. Interestingly Tom lit a roll up before the circle and if you don't draw a breath on a roll up they go out. The meditation lasted about twenty minutes and Tom's roll up was still alight. Lewis remarked the glow from the cigarette caught his eye and that it intensified on occasion as if it were being smoked. This experience was a first for Tina, our historian, and although she did not receive any form of messages she did enjoy the relaxing meditation. My experience was not what I wanted it to be. I seemed to be lying on my back in a narrow brick tunnel. I did hear voices and there was only one I recognised but he had nothing to do with the pub building. Lewis was unable to meditate at all due to the fact he was monitoring everybody else. Nobody else experiences anything during the meditation. We decided to do one last investigation of the building and allowed people to go off individually or in pairs. I thought Judy would explore upstairs again as she had already picked up on something and hopefully she would explore this further. Lewis accompanied her and the remaining people rearranged the tables and sat in the bar by the fire where I had felt activity earlier. The problem for Judy and her sister was they grew up in the village and their knowledge became a hindrance to them on the investigation rather than a helpful tool. I tried to pick up on the feelings I had experienced, and I asked those seated around me to help with this by trying to sense things themselves. I started picking up on a lady seated by the fireplace with a small boy and a dog. I could actually visualise them in my mind. Tom confirmed the dog had been seen before and Lorna said the woman had also been seen. I could see the fireplace as it once looked and described it to Tom and Lorna who were able to confirm my thoughts. A discussion started as to our findings and it was agreed that upstairs we had experienced memories locked within the pub, and the same down in the bar. When we tried to contact spirit within the pub we were unable to and instead people picked up on things seemingly unrelated to the building. Judy came back down stairs followed by Lewis and reported they were unable to pick up anything. The evening ended and we drifted off home with memories of an interesting evening.

The White Hart is haunted, but only by memories of past events .
Thanks Tom.

Ghosts of St Giles Street

Before we go into this next story I should like to point out the business name and location have been changed to protect the identity of the owner.

In the town of Northampton many old buildings have strange tales to tell. They have seen generations of families live their lives from beginning to end, and sometimes beyond. I was invited to join my old friends from the Northampton Paranormal Group on an investigation they were undertaking. In fact their investigation of this building has been a mammoth task in both time and complexity. This group has come a long way from its formation about six years ago and the group has grown in knowledge and understanding along the way. Founder member Emma Whiteman allows the group to take a relaxed and considered approach to their investigations, and this approach was certainly needed in this case.

The photo above shows members of the Northampton Paranormal Group. From left to right, Robin, Mandy, Mark, Emma, me, and Denis on the right.

The building we were going into has stood in the centre of Northampton since the great fire of 1675. There was a wooden building on the site before this date but we do not know what it was used for. One interesting place when investigating buildings that were once burnt down is the cellar. They are usually original to the former structure and can hold a wealth of information. Luckily Emma and her group had been investigating this building for more than four years so for me it was more of an information gathering evening, with a few experiments thrown in.

I began by asking Emma if her group had been able to find any history about the existing building and its occupants. They had discovered the building was once a large family home for a family with five or six children. The fact the family could afford a nanny infers wealth and success. Interestingly tales that the nanny disliked children was something that intrigued me. There were other facts about the family that Emma wanted to keep to herself until the end of the evening because they would influence the thoughts of people with us that evening. I should just explain that on this investigation we had a documentary film crew with us. They were following me around for a few months to gain an insight into the world of the paranormal and to film how I did investigations for my books. I wanted them to join in and take part, after all the best way to learn about anything is to actually do it. The facts that Emma withheld from us would be crucial to understanding the ghostly activity that was experienced by people within the building quite regularly.

I wanted to show Emma's group a slightly different approach to investigating than they were used to. Sometimes by helping people use their mind to explore residual energy left in a building from past residents you can glean more information. It has proven to be a very successful technique in the past. I would also be using the old and trusted pendulum in sand to see if people could influence its movement throughout the evening.

We were shown around the building by the group and I was surprised how vast it was. We started at the cellar, and from what I could see I would date some of the rooms to pre Victorian, and others looked as though they were from the Victorian time. There was a small kitchen and washroom with a brick built, fire heated boiler for washing, even the old wash dolly was there. There was a larger room and several small storage rooms. It looked as though there had been access to the building next door at one time, a bricked up archway being the clue. Up to the next floor and modernisation had wiped away all clues to its past use. Then up to the next floor using one of the two staircases, one either end of the building. Again this floor had been modernised with kitchens, living rooms, bedrooms, and bathrooms. Up to the top floor now and we found even more bedrooms, and a corridor that led across the building and down to the staircase on the far side. It seemed as though the whole house was split into two halves that mirrored each other. Now we had an idea of the layout is was important to identify hotspots of activity, natural or unnatural. Lewis used his meters and did a sweep of the building looking for electrical wiring and so on. I wanted to find out who among the group had experienced things in the past and in which part of the building. I wanted to take the person back to the spot and test their senses. I did the usual emotion tests, and I also did the Expanded Memory Recall test that has been so successful in the past. Mandy was willing to participate in the experiments at known hotspots so off we went to the living room on the first floor. On the way there I distinctly heard a little girl giggling as we reached the first landing. Mandy also heard it and said it was someone they had heard before.

Time for the test. I wanted Mandy to do the telekinesis through emotion test. In this test you are simply trying to move a pendulum located somewhere in the building with just the power of the mind. Experience has taught us that emotion is the best way to move an object. But this experiment is extremely difficult to perform and success is rare. Just two percent of people have had an effect on the pendulum in the last three years. We started with Fear, then onto Anger and finished with Joy. If you do this experiment with a friend please always finish with joy as the last emotion, it leaves people with a fond memory from the test. I was watching the time that each emotion was being experienced and had set the time the pendulum had been set up so we would know if the pendulum moved at a specific time we would know what emotion is likely to have caused it to move. I think Mandy found the experiment surprisingly difficult but performed it better than most that have tried. I asked her who she thought on the male side of the group would be good at the experiment and she said Robin would be a good candidate. A short while later Robin was making himself comfortable on the settee in front of me and the experiment began. It was exactly the same as Mandy's experiment but it lasted a shorter time. Men seem to be less intense than woman when bringing emotions to the fore. Women seem mentally more able to focus emotion and express their feelings, while men are reluctant to let go, maybe it is a fear of what would happen.

After Robin had completed the test I went down to the cellar where I had set the pendulum up in front of a video camera to see if it had moved. It had moved and in a curious way. If you hit or tap a pendulum suspended with its tip in sand it will draw circles and oval shapes as it rotates. The movement this pendulum had made was a straight line from the centre point, off to one side and back to the centre, only in one direction as if it had moved out and directly back to the start position. That movement can't be replicated naturally; I have tried to do it since that evening but the pendulum always swings back through the start position. I went back through the footage to see if anyone had touched it but there were no signs of anyone tampering with it at all. There was a movement at the time Mandy was going through the anger emotion but it was so fast you could barely see it.

The photo above shows the movement in the sand.

When people say it's coincidental that the pendulum moves at the time someone is mentally trying to move it, then yes that is a possibility. But the shapes the pendulum makes on the occasions we do the tests are extraordinary. This experiment is done, to test two things, can we move objects with the mind, and to show that when people report poltergeist activity during a haunting it's not necessarily spirits that are having an effect on their surroundings, people can as well.

Now I wanted to see if the group could tune into the energy of past residents of the building using the Extended Memory Recall method. From reading the other stories you know how this works. They look around for two to three minutes and then shut their eyes. Then they are asked to bring the room back into their mind's eye and allow their mind to fill the room with whatever and whoever they like, allowing their mind to run free. The results we have had over the years have been extremely interesting to say the least. As we were the people running the experiment we would normally find out as much history about a place as possible and then see if peoples can pick up on past events or people within a given location. Yes it is true to say the members of the group did know some of the history, but not all of it. I was looking for specifics in identifying people and times in history, christian, and surnames, how a person is dressed and so on. I decided to do two sessions, splitting the group in two. I asked the first group to visualise the room and so on. After a while I asked each person to tell us what they had seen. The results were very interesting but nothing out of the ordinary. But it was the second group that had made things really interesting. Some had brought memories of friends into the room, and others had trouble seeing anything at all, but then someone, I won't say who, began describing a room with a desk to the corner with a chaise longue to the side. There was a man seated at the desk, he seemed tall even when seated, with a pointed beard, a military looking man with a stiff starched collar. The viewer said she thought he seemed to be shouting at her in anger. He left the room and a lady entered and made the viewer laugh. Interestingly when I asked the viewer how tall she thought she was, she misunderstood the question and gave the answer as if I had not asked about the woman who had come into the room, but asked the question about herself. She said she thought she had been a child when viewing the room. Now this has never happened before. The viewer had placed herself into a character within the room and not simply observed, she had indeed entered into the event, superb! The exciting bit of this experiment was another person from the group had seen exactly the same thing, right down to the colour and type of curtains. Coincidence or imagination. I doubt that either could be as specific. The problem in doing this experiment was the prior knowledge the group had. I wanted to show the group how experiments like this can help in a long term investigation such as theirs. My hope is they use it on further investigations they do.

Each time we moved to a different location in the building and used the staircase we could hear the sound of a man whistling and the voice of a little girl giggling, or in conversation with someone. The only words during part of her conversation I caught were, "Not again". I asked Emma if they had heard these voices before and she explained that a young girl had jumped to her death from a window in a back bedroom onto the courtyard below after being raped by someone in her family. A man had also hung himself from the banister of the first staircase. In fact on one of their previous investigations in the building they were walking up the staircase talking about the man that hung himself there and one member of the group had remarked how dark it was, instantly the lights began to flicker. Here are some more reports from NPG during their stay within the building.

When sitting in the basement Emma was overcome with emotion and started crying for no reason. I also had the back of my neck touched, and then when we were on the first landing, team members heard a woman's whimper or cry. And when we were in the back bedroom on level 2, I felt very wary like there was someone else in there apart from us. Other group members saw shadows and we all heard footsteps above us.

I will now tell you who and what happened there. A girl called Alice, who was about 16/17 years old, was being sexually abused by her father and when she found out she was pregnant she could not deal with it, and telling her parents was not an option so she jumped to her death from her bedroom window which is the room at the back on level 2. Recently people have seen her in the courtyard at the back and they said she had no eyes, so they call her the girl with no eyes. Filled with remorse her father hung himself from the first staircase. We find the place very interesting, and every time we investigate we always get something whether it's a small sound or something different, the building always has a story to tell through the spirits that reside there.

Now remember I mentioned the documentary crew that were filming us that night. Well I wanted them to experience things for themselves, so I turned the tables on them. I asked them to try to do the Extended Memory Recall experiment while we were all down in the cellar, we would record their findings. I won't mention their names to protect their anonymity. I will simply call them J, and M. J went first and is a young man of about twenty. In his mind he saw large barrels in the room and people dashing about in a rush, stressed or scared of something. They wore long flowing dresses and seem to be trying to complete tasks in a short time. M's turn now, she is a young lady in her late teens early twenty's. M saw outside the cellar and could see a man in the room above sitting in the corner writing. She saw a bicycle to one side of the room, and then a little girl came in and asked if she could make cakes, she was told to go over to a corner and read a book. M described the girl as small and with brown hair. M was focusing more on the man reading the book. Both members of the crew found the experience enjoyable and it is something they had never tried before.

Now I did something I said I would never do. In the past people had badgered me to use a Ouija Board, and up to now I had refused. However, the people around me, with the exception of the film crew, were all experienced investigators and knew the risks involved. When I say risks, I mean they knew how to interpret any information that may come to light. It's the interpretation that many people get wrong, and it's that misinterpretation that scares them. Both Lewis and I had witnessed many Ouija Board sessions over the years and saw countless fraudulent attempts to hoodwink people. Well this session would be on the level and filmed for good measure. The board was set out and Lewis sat one side and I the other. I began by inviting the spirits within the building to join us and to take part in our investigation by answering simple questions about themselves. We placed our index fingers on the pointer and asked the questions. At first there were tiny movements but neither Lewis nor I could say that it wasn't involuntary movements from us causing this. It is extremely hard to hold your arm out and gently touch a pointer without moving it, fatigue sets in really fast. We then spotted another problem. As our arms got tired we rested our fingers on the pointer, this created weight that stopped any movement from occurring. I debated with the people watching that if a spirit was supposed to move the glass using our energy they would have a problem because of the weight our fingers had on the pointer. The only way the pointer was going to move is if we were channelling spirit through one of us, but that was not the objective. So if a spirit was in the room surely it could move the pointer without us touching it, simply by using the energy of the people in the room.

While some believers in the paranormal think movement on a Ouija board must be by spirit, it is a possibility that unconscious movements of those controlling the pointer is the culprit, a psychophysiological phenomenon known as the ideomotor effect. People simply scare themselves, and while this in itself isn't harmful, when there are people in the group who are susceptible to suggestion things can get out of hand and go horribly wrong. I had had enough of the Ouija board and suggested we get back to the investigation at hand.

I wanted to conduct a lights out circle in the cellar to see if we could contact the spirits. Lewis came up with the idea that he should go up to the Ouija Board and the people in the cellar try to get the spirits to move the glass upstairs, then he would try to get the spirits to do something to the people down in the cellar. I know it sounds odd but it has worked for us in the past. We gave Lewis fifteen minutes to settle down and we began inviting the spirits to join with us. It wasn't long before the temperature in the cellar plummeted with a recognisable difference. Then the footsteps on the stairway started. We all heard movement outside the door. The door itself let a small amount of light in top and bottom so when we saw movement via shadows outside the door we immediately thought it was Lewis larking about but on investigation Lewis was still upstairs. We continued the circle and again we could sense movement. This time the movement was inside the room close to Emma and me. The shadows seem to be small children darting about the room. Was it our imagination? Emma felt as though she wanted to cry and the emotion she felt seemed stronger than on previous investigations.

Lewis came down and asked how we got on. He had been trying to get the spirits to have an effect on of us in some way, I think that worked. He said nothing happened with the board upstairs, and to be honest I wasn't surprised.

Everything that happened to us that evening seemed to point to one thing. Energy from traumatic events is still circulating within the building and is experienced by the people working there. It is the classic haunting and one that repeats itself across the country. I think Emma believes there is also a spirit entity residing within the building paying penance for his past crimes. It is possible a spirit still wanders the staircase looking for forgiveness from a girl who once trusted him. What do you believe?

Ghosts in the Bear

In the town of Northampton, at the top of The Drapery and the start of Sheep Street stands the Bear public house. At the time of writing this story the Fish Market to the rear of the pub is being demolished and a new bus terminus is to replace it. The Bear is another of Northampton's old pubs and has tales of ghosts going back for many years. It's a popular pub for locals and has a warm welcome for the traveller. A survey of the land underneath the pub found what experts estimate could be the remains of an ancient synagogue, dating back hundreds of years. This intrigued me so I went to the pub to join a visit by a Northampton history group. I thought it was a good idea to have a look around and to see for myself if the tales I had heard actually held any truth. I was there with Lewis trying to keep a low profile to simply join the group and to learn as much as possible. However, the best laid plans don't always go according to plan and we were soon being asked about the investigations we had done in the town. They thought we were planning to investigate the pub and wanted to be involved. What we do fascinates people and it does not matter if you are at a party, wedding, or even simply going to the pub, people want to hear your stories. This occasion was no different and we had to tell them what we were doing and that we were not planning an overnight investigation. This helped a little and we were able to join in on the tour of the property. The group were trying to learn as much as they could about the structure of the building and how it was used in its early years. The cellar was the best way to see the early structure and it was there we were taken to. It seemed to be a regular cellar and of the many cellars Lewis and I had seen it was not strikingly different. There was however one strange structure that started a debate about its use and why it was in the position it was. To the front wall that led under the path of the street outside was a staircase. Now you may be thinking this is not unusual and it was simply a means to get to the cellar from outside. But why would you want to do that? The old barrel shoot is there and pub cellars are accessed from the bar so why a staircase. There are tales of footsteps being heard on the staircase while people were working in the cellar and barrels have been moved and restacked. The staff had also reported seeing a tall shadow drifting in and out of the cellar rooms.

The staircase leading nowhere in the cellar of the Bear.
Well-worn steps show they have seen many years of use, but why.

I wanted to know more about what people had seen and experienced in the pub so after the group had debated the use of the stairs and the other rooms I decided to talk to the landlady about their experiences. She began by telling a story about her middle son who worked in the pub. At the end of the evening when everyone had gone he would play a game of pool to help unwind, but he began to see people, or more specifically the movement of people out the corner of his eye. He would be playing a shot and would see someone walk by the table as he went to strike the ball. This went on for weeks and he eventually said to his mother, "I can't do this anymore, the place is packed with people moving about while I am playing". The landlady said she would often sit playing the slot machine of an evening but never on her own. She would only play on it when one of her children or her husband was in the bar. The reason was, one night when she was totally alone in the pub she sat at the machine playing and she felt someone blow on the back of her neck and it totally freaked her out. Even now when she has someone with her it can sometimes happen, but having someone there helps her deal with it. She is always the last person down in the pub at night and always locks the cellar door; she said she hates locking the door as it feels evil, as if something from hell is about to burst through it. Her sister and brother-in-law came to stay at the pub and had travelled down from Scotland arriving about one thirty in the morning. His father was very ill and had been taken into hospital and he was unsure whether to come down or stay in Scotland just in case he was needed. As they were going up and down the stairs taking in their suitcases her brother-in-law felt someone place a hand firmly on his shoulder. He moved to one side saying sorry pal, thinking someone wanted to get by but there was nobody there. Five minutes later the phone rang to say his father had passed away.

I asked the landlady if the activity happening within the pub was things being seen, or being heard, or things actually being moved about. She said it was physical movement of objects that seemed to be the main activity, glasses and chairs in the bar and barrels in the cellar. Unfortunately the landlady was about to hand the pub over to new owners a few days after our visit so we were unable to do an in-depth investigation, maybe sometime in the future though. We did not have time to do a full history of this pub because of the sheer workload of other cases, but if you are travelling to Northampton stop off and visit the Bear public house and see what you think of the atmosphere, you may feel a hand on your shoulder, or see a fleeting glimpse of someone by the pool table. Enjoy.

Interviews

I like to interview people who join me on investigation to find out a little more about how they interpret the subject of ghosts and spirits. It's also a way of showing you that we do not exclude the sceptic, and in some circumstances their input is vital to maintain a well-balanced investigation.

Interview with Tina, (Team historian).

I began by asking Tina, when we are on an investigation what is she looking for specifically. She explained that she often checks out the history of the location well in advance of our visits. While there she often talks to locals to gather more information. Local knowledge can be very informative. Tina is intrigued with stories of ghosts and spirits and said that people telling her such stories whole heartedly believe what they had seen was real. She went on to say that she does not believe anything will happen to her while on investigations with us and that it is the history that she concentrates on. She would like to have more time to look into the family history of clients to be able to tell them a little of their ancestry. I then asked Tina if she believed in ghosts. Her reply was, "Still unsure".

I like the fact I can work with people who are not afraid to say what they think and give honest answers. While on investigations Tina is unaffected by paranormal mysticism and just gets on with the job in hand, and that's what you want when searching for the truth.

Interview with Emma Whiteman, founder of Northampton Paranormal.

Emma started the Northampton Paranormal Group in April 2007. A few days later she had nearly twenty members, such was the interest in the paranormal at that time. The popularity of the group took her by surprise and I think it fair to say she was a little shocked. Over the next two years they did some extremely interesting investigations. But with any successful group as time goes on people want different things and decide to do things on their own. Emma knew this was a possibility and the group slimmed down to a more manageable size and began to investigate locations that were more welcoming of smaller groups. The team also changed how they approached investigations. They had learnt through experience that people expected a professional, and a more structured approach. Two more years went by and the strain of constantly searching haunted locations had taken the energy from the whole group, they needed a break. I can sympathise with that, I had to do it myself. Emma and the team took a year off and have now come back reenergised and ready to do more work. After meeting the group on an investigation, told earlier in the book. I was really pleased to see how much they had changed. It's easy to get disheartened and to lose interest in this work. Perseverance will reward people who stick at it and refuse to give up.

As for future plans, Emma said the group will remain small and go on investigations that test them. It's a hobby, and hobbies should be enjoyable. But she did add that she was looking for that one investigation that would push the group to the limit. I suppose it's like every hobby, you are always looking for the ultimate thrill.

Interview with Lewis Dellar, (Team Parapsychologist).

I began by asking Lewis how his approach has changed regarding investigations. He explained that he feels he is more open minded, especially over the last two years. Not in a belief sense, but more in an acceptance of the way other people perform their investigations. Lewis said in the past he was very regimented in his approach and would not waver from his set pattern no matter what. But he realised that this subject is plagued by extremes, both in belief and lack of belief, there seems to be no middle ground just a constant war between the two separate sections. This is something he wanted to tackle starting with his own unwavering approach to investigations; you need to be able to react to different circumstances. Lewis went on to explain where his beliefs were on sensitive's and mediums, although they have not changed radically he does now believe they have a place on investigations and the information they get should be looked into. He is interested in the accuracy of some of the information he seems to be coming out with on investigations. He has been surprised how accurate he has been but feels it is more coincidental and puts it down to his creative imagination rather than any spiritual gift. It is however intriguing, and he believes that over time he has become more in tune to environmental forces. It's like anything, the more you do the better you get. He does believe he is still learning and it is a very steep learning curve he is on. Learning the basis of physics and mechanics behind the experiences people are having is all well and good, but it still boils down to the fact that you are still relying on somebody's eye witness testimony to say they have seen, heard, or felt something. He went on to say his views would now be that the future of investigating the paranormal from his perspective is through neurology and he would like to spend more time in studying the chemical reaction in peoples brain during their experiences. If there was a way to push the subject forward, to find out if the things they are experiencing are hallucinogenic based or are physically in front of the person. He said we need to know what the brain is doing during such experiences. Lewis believes that is one thing the paranormal researcher has left out, partly through funding and partly because the other avenues seem to be such strong contenders, faith and commercial gain. It's a multi-million pound business to have a haunted location these days and to supply gadgets to investigators. It has made it extremely difficult for us doing confidential investigations because we all get tarred with the same brush. Lewis stated that this is the most fascinating but the most frustrating subject he has ever been involved with because it is so hit and miss and so disjointed. You are dealing with an existence that can never be proven either way.

In all the years we have been working together, are we any closer to answering the question, "Is there an existence after death?" We cannot say either way. But we will keep on trying.

Note from the Author.

I hope you have found this book an interesting read, and one that has given you food for thought. All I can do is try to give people information. How you interpret the information is for you to decide. Until next time, have fun with your search for the truth.

Adrian.